MY LIFE IN THE FOREIGN LEGION

MY LIFE IN THE FOREIGN LEGION

BY

PRINCE AAGE OF DENMARK

THE BATTERY PRESS
Nashville

In Association With
ARTICLES OF WAR, LTD
Skokie

Originally published 1928
Reprinted by
THE BATTERY PRESS
P.O. Box 198885
Nashville, Tennessee 37219
First in The European Wars Series
1994
ISBN: 0-89839-196-2
Printed in the United States of America

PART I

~ RIF WAR NORTHERN FRONT ~ — — — French Outpost Line

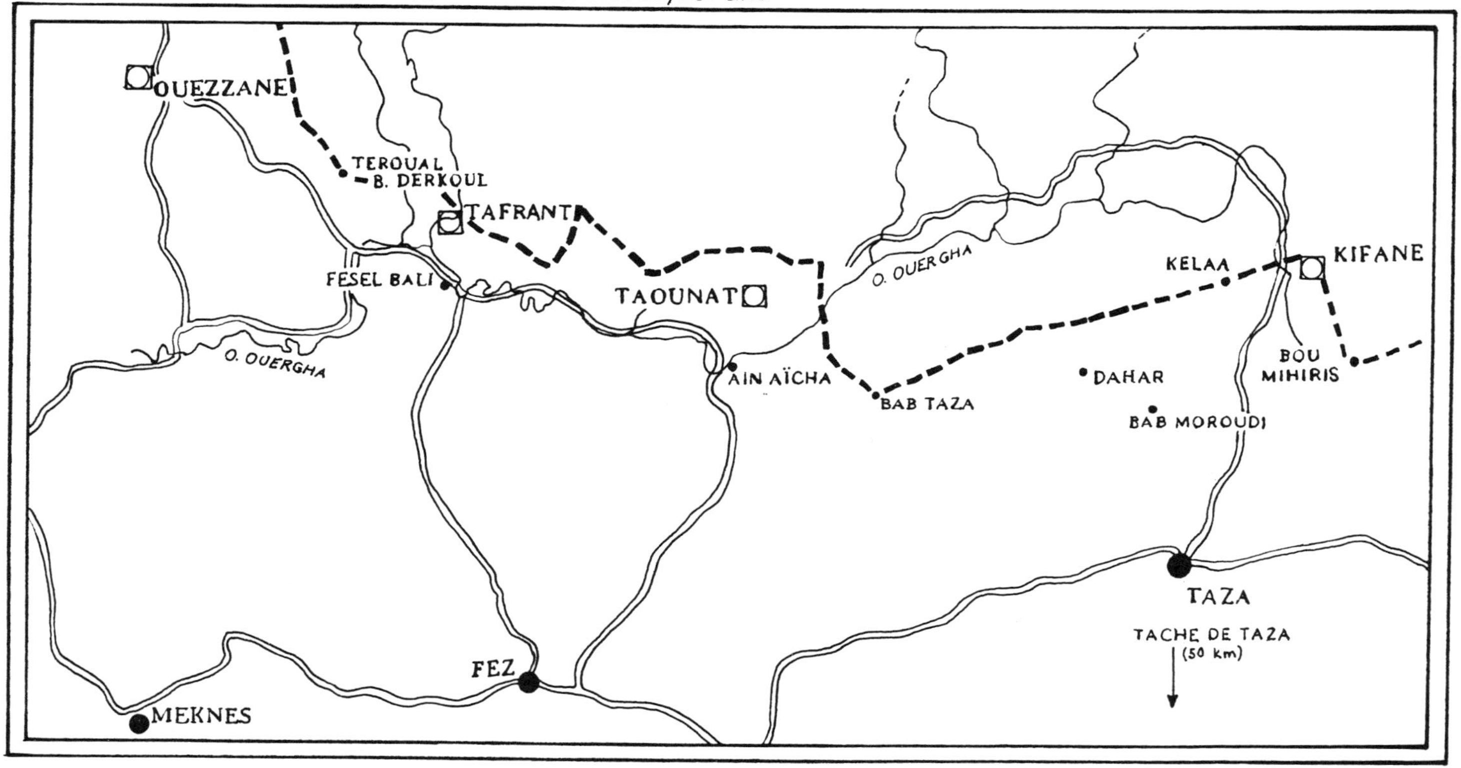

MY LIFE IN THE FOREIGN LEGION

CHAPTER ONE

I

WE were fifteen at the mess, a heterogeneous group, bound to fellowship by our common profession of soldiering. Almost every arm was represented: a colonel of Spahis—the brilliant native cavalry—several captains and a major of infantry, two gunners, a captain of the Foreign Legion, and a flyer. A major of the British Army, travelling for pleasure, and I, a neophyte Légionnaire, completed the roster.

It was the evening of our third day at sea. To-morrow we would land at Casablanca and, from there, go on to join our various regiments. I drew aside my fellow Légionnaire and questioned him concerning the famous force which I was about to join.

"Do you happen to know Major M——?" asked the Captain. "He is typical of the Legion."

I replied in the negative, and he went on: "M—— is one of the two or three commissioned Légionnaires who managed to survive the World War. I speak of him to you because I consider him the beau-ideal of what an officer should be. He is hard, hard as nails; but to look at him you would never suspect it. He is quite handsome, so well groomed as to verge upon foppishness, and peculiarly gentle in his speech. Unfailingly courteous to his subordinates, he is the strictest of disciplinarians. The men know his courage, and respect him."

The Captain paused and lit a cigarette. "Major M—— makes it a point," he continued, "never to be armed. He claims that, in the first place, an officer should set an example rather than fight, and that, in the second, the weight of a revolver causes one's belt to sag and thus spoils the set of one's tunic.

"Some three months ago, the Major, at the head of his battalion, was making his way through a pass in the Middle Atlas Mountains.

Suddenly, there came a withering burst of rifle fire, and, before you could say 'knife,' the tribesmen were upon them. M—— rallied his shaken forces, took up a prominent position, and calmly directed operations with his walking stick. When the crucial moment came, he led a charge. For a while, it was anybody's fight, and M—— was everywhere at once, up and down the line, his voice rising, occasionally, above the snap of rifles. Finally, the bayonet, in the hands of trained soldiery, began to tell. The Berbers broke and ran, but not before three or four of them had engaged M—— simultaneously and cut him down. His men found him later, badly wounded, his right hand grasping the shattered walking stick."

"Will he live?" I inquired.

"But certainly!" answered the Captain. "It takes more than a few knife wounds to do for a Légionnaire."

I pondered the story for a few moments, and then asked, "Is there any bit of advice you can give me as to my conduct in the Legion?"

"Yes," said the Captain. "In the Legion, when you are not quite certain you can accomplish a thing, give your word of honour. When you *are* quite certain, make a bet!"

Next morning, I was up at dawn. It was with mixed emotions that I contemplated, from the steamer's deck, the white walls of Casablanca rising out of the bay. From our position, some two miles offshore, it appeared a dream city; its Moorish domes and arches, its graceful minarets etched against the sky, gleaming like marble in the intense African sunlight, lent the place that unreal air of romance with which the Occidental observer comes naturally to associate the World of Islam. There, like some enormous pearl in a baroque setting, lay the town, the base port of the French Armies in Morocco.

Almost since boyhood I had cherished an aspiration to become, one day, a soldier of the Legion. Those of us in Denmark who follow the profession of arms have had little opportunity, in recent years, for any actual fighting, and it has become a custom for some of the more adventurous of our officers to seek service with the armies of other nations. The most famous, of course, of all modern military bodies is the French Légion d'Étrangère, and many a good Dane has found his death beneath the tricolour on the torrid sands or windswept heights of northern Africa. Naturally, then, as a youth, I turned my thoughts to the Legion, but because of my family I had little hope of ever being in a position to carry out my ambition.

In 1909, at the age of nineteen, I entered the army of Denmark, and for the next few years was kept busy learning my profession. In 1913, I received my commission as sub-lieutenant in the regiment of Royal Life Guards, with which organization I continued to serve until 1922 when I resigned as a captain.

During the years intervening I welcomed every opportunity for foreign service. The life in a Guards regiment, amusing enough for a while, soon begins to pall with its endless repetition of formalities and state functions. I was ever eager to put behind me my courtier's duties in order that I might gain experience at the work I loved best. Therefore, it was with ill-concealed joy that I accepted an appointment, late in 1913, as military observer to the Greek forces, then engaged in hostilities against Bulgaria.

Shortly after my return from Greece, I was again given an opportunity to serve abroad and, during the World War, was on duty for one year with the Italian Army, where I again acted as observer. In 1919, I was appointed a member of the military commission sent to France, England, and the United States, and it was during this period that I had my first opportunity to observe the conduct and organization of America's splendid troops. Later, I spent a year with the French in Metz, and there learned something of the customs and traditions which were to become so familiar to me as an officer of the Foreign Legion. Upon the completion of this mission I returned to Copenhagen and once more took up my duties in the Royal Life Guards.

You may well imagine the distaste with which I began again the old familiar round of parades, manœuvres, reviews, and inspections. The last several years, filled with fresh experiences and adventures, had ill fitted me for garrison life. Once more my thoughts were turned toward the Legion. Away back in 1912, there had been, as senior lieutenant of my company, an officer who had served with the Foreign Legion for six years. I recalled now the many tales of adventure with which he had been wont to regale me during the long tedious days we spent on duty together. Then, too, there were several officers stationed at Copenhagen who had spent periods of from six months to a year with the famous force, and these men never tired of relating their experiences to me; nor I, in truth, of hearing them.

Finally, my desire crystallized itself into action and, circumstances being favourable, I applied to the French Military attaché at Copenhagen for a commission in the Légion d'Étrangère. My first step, of course, upon learning that I would be accepted, had been to resign my commission in the Guards; and so, when I received my appointment on December 28, 1922, little remained for me to do but to arrange my luggage and obtain passports, before I was off for Paris in search of equipment.

I left Paris at eight o'clock of an evening early in February, 1923. Attired in the uniform of France, I felt rather constrained and ill at ease, but this feeling soon wore off and, ere many days had passed, I was as much at home in this new uniform as if I had been wearing it all my life. Arriving at Marseilles, I reported at the Town Major's office, and, after a few formalities, was ordered to take ship for Casablanca, one of Morocco's seaports, situated on the Atlantic coast some three hundred miles south-west of Gibraltar.

II

In A.D. 787, there was a battle at Fakh, near Mecca in Arabia. Fought between the descendants of the Caliph Ali (son-in-law of the Prophet Mohammed) and the armies of Al-Hadi, Caliph of Baghdad, it is said that its cause was the intemperance of some members of the House of Ali. These gentlemen, it is recorded, transgressed the laws of the Prophet to the extent that they partook too freely of wine, for which offence they were punished by being paraded through the streets of the Holy City with halters strung about their necks. Honour demanded satisfaction, and, in the battle which ensued, the cohorts of the noble Ali received it in full measure, together with a drubbing of no mean proportions.

Although the slaughter was great, there emerged from the conflict one Idris Ben Abd Allah, the man whose destiny it was to found the new Islamic empire of the West. Making his escape with the aid of a faithful slave, Idris wandered for more than two years, ever westward, arriving, finally, at the thriving town of Ouilili in the centre of northern Morocco. Here he fell in with the Aouraba tribe—one of those already converted to Islam—and made himself known to them as a descendant of the Prophet. This circumstance, coupled with what must have been a remarkable flair for leadership, aided Idris in the furtherance of his ambition. He married a woman of the tribe, one Kanza, and before long was chosen as its chief.

For three years and one month, Idris reigned, governing wisely and extending his influence over the whole of Morocco. For the most part, his was a peaceful era, although there were occasional clashes with the wilder Berber tribesmen—men whose direct descendants we have been fighting in recent years.

Idris was assassinated, finally, at the instigation of his old enemy the Caliph of Baghdad, but not before he had produced a son and heir who was to extend the sphere of his influence. He died to become the national saint of Morocco; but his son lived to found the city of Fez and to carve out an empire very similar in extent to the Morocco of to-day.

The present Morocco has about the same area as France. Its northern and western frontiers are, respectively, the Mediterranean and the Atlantic Ocean; Algeria lies to the east, while the great desert of the Sahara forms an impregnable southern bulwark. The country is characteristically rugged and mountainous, excellently adapted to banditry and guerilla warfare, and a breeding place for hardy, aggressive men. The Riff mountains, which run east and west in parallel chains, are in the extreme northern sector of the country. Farther south, the Middle Atlas range renders the terrain virtually impassable, and in the distant south the Great Atlas Mountains extend away into the desert.

The great valleys between the mountain ranges are well watered by many rivers and, consequently, are fertile to a surprising degree.

During the harvest, the country is one waving sea of cereals.

The French interest in Morocco is not, of course, purely altruistic. The country's vast natural wealth has scarcely been exploited as yet, although government geologists have discovered iron, copper, lead, and even an occasional deposit of gold in the mountains. It is to be expected that these and other discoveries will prove of immense value in the years to come. I have not heard of any oil being found in the country, yet it is not improbable that in this field also the geologists have recorded finds and filed them for future reference.

Up to the present date, the greatest single source of revenue to France has been the enormous phosphate deposits, the exploitation of which began in 1917. Four hundred thousand tons of this valuable substance were exported during the year of 1924.

It will be readily appreciated, then, that, in addition to its purely political worth to France, Morocco is an immensely valuable granary and potential source of raw materials for a country which, more and more, is given over to manufacturing and commercial pursuits.

It is, in a sense, unfortunate for the French that the inhabitants of Morocco have preserved their racial integrity and their common tongue. Although, as I have explained, the tribesmen embraced the Islamic faith centuries ago, they have never permitted the foreigner to impose his civilization upon them. Looking back through the ages, one finds that Phœnicians, Carthaginians, and Romans, one after the other, endeavoured to conquer and colonize the country. Later, in the Seventh Century, the Arab hordes swept in from the East and overran Morocco for a time. Yet the Moors remain, their Berber blood virtually uncontaminated, while a few crumbling ruins mark the futile conquests of erstwhile great civilizations.

Now it is the French who pin their hopes of empire upon Morocco's future, and it is not unreasonable to suppose that they too will eventually go the way of their predecessors.

Political prediction, however, is not within the province of this book. My own experience in Morocco has convinced me that France has governed the country wisely and well. Internal policy is left pretty much in the hands of the Sultan; foreign affairs have not suffered from the direction of Lyautey; without attempting to westernize the country, the French administration has introduced modern agricultural and marketing methods which have vastly increased the national prosperity. Whatever the outcome, the French mandate has been of incalculable value to Morocco in that it has enabled a backward, tyrant-ridden country to take its place in the modern world.

Of the Spanish mandate over northern Morocco I cannot speak so highly. The Spaniard, throughout history, has been a notoriously inept colonizer, and his adminstration in Africa has not proved an exception to the rule. It is doubtful if Spain would continue to exercise its costly mandate were it not for the diplomatic pressure of Great Britain. England, it will be remembered, holds Gibraltar, and it is no part of her plan to allow the Mediterranean to become a French lake. Thus it is that the diplomatic chess game of the great powers can neutralize the most sincere efforts of colonial administrators.

Of the several important Moroccan cities, Fez, in the north, is perhaps the most interesting from the historical standpoint, while Marakeech (or Marakesh), in the extreme south, is the most beautiful. Rabat, it is true, has a certain exotic charm of its own; Meknes is desolate, and Casablanca is a dirty, modern seaport, more typical of Europe than of Africa.

The city of Fez lies at the head of a deep valley where the river Fez leaves off its wanderings along the flat plain of Sais to hurry steeply downward towards its rendezvous with the Sebou, four or five kilometres below. In the annals of the city it is written that Omeir, minister of Idris II, explored the plain of Sais in search of a suitable spot upon which to rear a capital for his master's newly formed state. At first, he was inclined to select the Springs of Ras El Ma (the source of the river, about eight miles above the present Fez), but mature deliberation convinced him that the more protected situation in the valley was better adapted to defence.

Approaching the town from the direction of Sais, one glimpses first the greyish line of ramparts presenting a formidable and imposing barrier across the entire head of the valley. Drawing nearer, one is further impressed by these walls, which are impregnable to anything short of modern siege artillery.

Finally, the triple arch of Bab Segma is reached, the first great gateway of Fez. Its three arches, differing slightly in form, present a threatening exterior, well in keeping with the might of the Sultans, and calculated to strike terror into the hearts of enemies who have come to spy out the city's vulnerability. The lengthy approaches, shut in by walls of ever-increasing height, the vast esplanades growing gradually narrower and ending finally in sturdy gateways, dominated by towers and bastions, were intended to impress friend and foe alike, and to give them ample time to ponder the power behind the walls.

Beyond Bab Segma, one enters not the town but a great network of courts and passages, divided by fortified gates. This section, known as Fez Djedid or the New Fez, was built during the Thirteenth Century and is new only as regards the original city, farther down the valley. Fez Djedid is the seat of the municipal government and military power.

More courtyards and gateways, and then the passage begins to narrow. A final gateway

—of modern construction this time—and the abrupt descent into the city proper begins. The street is full of movement and colour. Shops appear beneath the houses on either side of the way. The centre of the town that is Morocco's glory, and a hotbed of intrigue, is at hand.

In the centre of Fez is the Kaiseria, a sort of super-market-place where most of the town's business is transacted. It consists of a number of narrow, shop-lined streets clustered about a tiny square where business men gather to discuss their affairs, to barter volubly for anything and everything, to sip their aromatic Turkish coffee, and, perhaps, to philosophize upon the ultimate downfall of the Infidel.

Fez is Morocco. Had we lost it during the Riff advance it is doubtful if we could have held on to the remainder of the country for much longer. Its significance to us is symbolical as well as strategical for, if once we show ourselves too weak to hold the town, the whole of Morocco, erstwhile friend and foe alike, will rise up in arms to overthrow the Roumi. And history supplies excellent precedent for the statement that when a whole people becomes thoroughly aroused even the strongest armies cannot prevail.

III

As we approached the landing stage at Casablanca, I thought of the possibilities, pleasant and unpleasant, with which my approaching adventure was fraught, spent some moments in fruitless conjecture as to the reception which I was likely to meet and, altogether, worked myself into a state of excitement which was, I think, pardonable in view of my decisive action from which, now, there could be no withdrawal.

After landing and seeing to my kit, I had little time to spend in an examination of Casablanca. At the wharves all was hustle and bustle—troops arriving, *permissionnaires* taking their departure, wagons and lorries loading and unloading; in short, all the ordered confusion that is the inevitable accompaniment of military expeditions. My white city of the morning had taken on, close up, a dingier aspect. My nostrils were assailed with an odour which I came, later, to associate with the meaner sections of all Oriental towns.

Orders required that I report to the Maréchal Lyautey at Rabat. Accompanied by my British friend, I engaged a motor, and we were soon speeding the ninety kilometres—on an excellent road, by the way—towards the City of the Sultan. At Rabat I reported to the Maréchal's Chief of Staff, who informed me that his superior was ill at Fez and that I should have to await his return. Then ensued an impatient fortnight during which I reported at the Residency not less than three times a day, and during which the Maréchal failed to put in his appearance. Finally, moved by my expostulations and pleadings, the Chief of Staff ordered me to join my regiment at Meknes and there, at last, I became a full-fledged Légionnaire.

Colonel Martin, commanding the Second Regiment of the Legion, was a man of some sixty years, very tall, straight, and stern-looking. His close-cropped hair fitted his head like a casque, and a wind-burnt, parchment-like complexion added to his forbidding appearance. I learned later that he had served with the

Legion for thirty years, that he was one of the finest officers in the army, and that he seldom opened his mouth except to issue a laconic order. His greeting was kind but brief, and a few moments later I found myself at the cantonment of the First Battalion, Second Regiment, ready to take up my duties.

During the next few weeks I spent my time in familiarizing myself with the regimental routine, in becoming acquainted with my brother officers, and in absorbing the peculiar atmosphere that permeates this "cohort of the damned." I learned, almost at once, that the first rule of the Legion is "no questions asked." A man there, officer or private, is judged by his deportment as a Légionnaire. The past is obliterated. It makes no difference whether your comrade in arms has been a pauper or a grand duke in civil life; in the Legion he is a soldier, and upon his ability as a military man his reputation rests.

Almost 60 per cent. of the Foreign Legion are Germans. I have no idea of the reason for this, except that they are the finest soldiers I have ever seen. Out of this fact, though, rises the popular conception of the Legion as a haven for cut-throats and criminals. Germany, naturally enough, is not anxious to send her young men to fight under the tricolour, and in order to combat wholesale enlistments, has organized a system of propaganda calculated to discourage men of the better type from joining the organization. In this she has succeeded in part, for while adventurous young Germans continue to flock to the French standard, the world at large seems to have gained the impression that the Legion is filled with thieves and cut-purses of the lowest type.

Let me say here that this is absolutely untrue. Many men there have been in the Legion who have joined under a cloud of one kind or another. Others have come in search of adventure, and others still because they are better fitted for fighting than for civilization. I have had, under me, the roughest kinds of men—and the finest. But never have I come across a true criminal type.

Some of you are doubtless familiar with the story of the young German who joined the Legion as a private several years before the World War. A quiet, unassuming fellow, he performed his duties faithfully for a considerable period until, suddenly, he was stricken with typhoid and sent to the base hospital at Algiers, where he died shortly afterwards. In going through his personal effects the hospital authorities were amazed to learn that the young soldier was Kaiser Wilhelm's nephew. The German consulate was notified immediately, and, a few days later, a warship put into Algiers and bore the body off in state.

Strange as this tale may seem, it is not particularly unusual to come across such cases in the Legion. In my own company I have had many enlisted men who, at some previous time, had been officers in one European army or another. In 1924, I found that a private soldier, serving under my command, was none other than a prince of the House of Bourbon. How he came to be there was none of my concern, and, indeed, I have never learned. It was sufficient for me to know that, as a soldier, he performed well.

My battalion was at that time commanded by a Major Büschenschütz, an Alsatian who had served with the Legion for many years. A little man, smartly turned out, he was a fine linguist, a graduate of the Staff College—one of the youngest—and the hero of many wild escapades. He had served in Russia and Siberia with the White Army of Admiral Kolchak, in Poland under Pilsudski, and in a dozen or more remote corners of the globe. As senior captain, I acted as the Major's adjutant, and he proved to be not only a good superior officer but a valuable friend. He spared himself no pains in instructing me at my new duties, going out of his way many times to confer upon me those small favours which go such a long way in making the hard life of a Légionnaire more bearable. One of the most valuable of his services was to assign, as my personal orderly, an old Légionnaire named Gerlech. This man, a native of Bavaria, had served in the Legion for twenty-two years, taking part in scores of battles and engagements. In 1907, he had aided in the storming of Casablanca, and, since then, had distinguished himself many times. Although a holder of the Médaille Militaire, the highest decoration for valour that an enlisted man can win, he had chosen to remain a private soldier, saying that, as a non-commissioned officer, he would have been too severe with the men.

Gerlech remained with me until 1924, and during the first year or so, I should have been lost without him. In a thousand little ways he contributed to my comfort. A stickler for etiquette, he would not allow my horse orderly to come near me, but insisted that all my requirements should be transmitted through him. He knew everyone in the Legion, officer or enlisted man, and could tell me exactly what to expect from those with whom I came in contact. He was the perfect servant in all but one respect. Upon the evening of pay day—which comes every fortnight—Gerlech would get drunk. Returning to my quarters, I would find my belongings in perfect order, boots polished, buttons glistening, and Gerlech's Médaille Militaire lying upon my writing table (for no Légionnaire wears his decoration if there is any possibility of his disgracing it; nor is a medal ever allowed to accompany its owner to the guard house). Twenty-four hours later, Gerlech would turn up again, perfectly groomed, in spotless uniform, but with eyes slightly bloodshot and a trifle puffy. Neither of us ever alluded to these lapses from grace, and the man knew well that he was perfectly safe so long as he did not overstep the bounds.

I kept Gerlech, as I have said, until the winter of 1924, when I was to lose him through a peculiarly tragic circumstance. It happened, that winter, that my wife had come to pay me a visit and was stopping at Rabat, while I was again stationed at Meknes, where I was instructing a class of neophyte machine gunners. It was my practice to run down each week-end to Rabat, accompanied by my orderly, and, once there, to turn him over to my wife's maid with instructions that he be well treated. With this woman, an Italian of uncertain age and singularly unattractive appearance, he struck up a warm friendship. He was unused, however, to the society of women; the kindness with which he was treated at first astonished and later troubled him. Twenty-odd years in the desert will do strange things to a man's mind, and there is no telling with what romantic fancies this new association filled his sun-parched being.

It was at about this time that I noticed a rapid and inexplicable decrease in my supply of eau-de-Cologne. I used quite a lot of the stuff to protect my skin from the sun and wind, yet it seemed strange that I should be obliged to purchase a new bottle almost every other day. I suspected Gerlech and watched him closely, but said nothing for fear of setting him off on some wild tangent. I feared the *cafard*, dread affliction of Legionnaires, which comes of too much sun and lonesomeness, combined with over-indulgence in the vile native fermentations. Touched by *cafard*, a man will do anything from bursting into tears to committing a brutal murder. I began to worry about my servant, and next week-end left him at Meknes while I journeyed to Rabat alone.

Returning on Sunday evening, I entered my quarters to find everything in disorder. Suspecting at once that something was amiss, I took a hasty inventory of my belongings and found that nothing had disappeared except my service revolver. Upon my writing table was a note, written in the execrable French of Gerlech. "My Captain," it said, "forgive me for having caused you so much trouble. You have been too good to me. I go to kill myself. Do not attempt to find me for I shall have hidden myself well."

My apprehensions, then, had been justified. I cursed myself for having left Gerlech alone, and then set about notifying the police and military, in an almost hopeless attempt to remedy what seemed to me to have been my negligence. I might have spared myself the effort for, despite the most assiduous search. no trace of the man was found.

Three weeks later, an Arab, riding in trom the desert, reported finding the body of a Légionnaire at the bottom of a coke oven some miles outside Meknes. I investigated at once and found poor Gerlech, in spotless uniform, ribbons pinned to his breast, a bullet hole drilled through his head. My revolver had been stolen by some native ghoul.

IV

It was at Meknes, then, in the spring of 1923, that I joined my battalion. A few weeks later, we received orders to proceed to the vicinity of the post Timhadit, about one hundred kilometres to the south-east, in the heart of the Middle Atlas range. There we were to act as a guard to transport and to protect existing supply bases; for a campaign was projected later in the spring against outlying Berber tribes which had not yet been subjected to the French régime. Upon the morning of departure, our orders being to march out at twelve-thirty, the Colonel invited the officers to luncheon. After an enjoyable meal, we joined our troops—who, by the way, had been paid early that morning—to find the men swaying in ranks. They had spent every last sou on liquor and were, almost to a man, hopelessly drunk. Accustomed to commanding the comparatively docile guardsmen, I was amazed at the sight of intoxicated soldiers drawn up on parade; later I learned that this was a practice almost customary in the Legion. Swallowing any comment, I mounted my native pony, my long legs dangling almost to the ground, and took up my post alongside Major Büschenschütz at the rear of the column.

What a march that was! The sun beat down mercilessly upon the alcohol-soaked Légionnaires, and before we had travelled a half-dozen kilometres, men began to drop out to the right and the left. The Major and I urged the stragglers on, dismounting after a while to throw a couple of almost insensible soldiers across our saddles like so many sacks of meal. We reached the bivouac at last, there to be greeted by our indignant orderlies, who had gone on ahead to pitch our tents. Gerlech, sober and self-righteous, read me a lecture on the impropriety of an officer's walking while a worthless drunkard rode. He dragged to the ground the poor sot carried by my pony, cursed and buffeted him a bit, and used his tunic as a rag to clean my saddle. A sad business, altogether.

The day's march sobered the troops. There was no more wine to be had, and the next morning we pushed towards the hills, camping that night at El Hajeb. The country through which we marched was exceedingly beautiful. The fields were a riot of multi-coloured wild flowers growing in lush luxuriance; ahead towered the mountains, their slopes grown thick with cedars, the heights crag-crowned, with occasional patches of snow reflecting the sun's rays in patterns of deep blue and white. It may be of interest to note here that the designs of the native rugs are copied from these fields, those manufactured in the low-lands rivalling the wild flowers in colour, while craftsmen who inhabit the hills are influenced by the more sombre hues of the peaks above them, and turn out their product in blues or blacks and white. Show me a Moorish rug and I will tell you the section of the country in which it was made.

We bivouacked the third night at the political post of Azrou, which was under the command of Major Neville, a nephew of the famous General. Here we were overtaken by a terrific thunderstorm, the violence of which I have never seen equalled. The temperature dropped forty degrees; black clouds gathered; ominously the thunder rolled, and it began to hail, stones the size of pigeon's eggs battering down on our shelter tents. The encampment was quickly flooded, no one had a dry stitch of clothing; and our blood, thinned out by the heat of the plains, congealed in our veins. For two hours we suffered, and then the storm ceased as quickly as it had begun. Camp fires flickered, piercing the black. The Major ordered a double ration of wine to be served out, and soon the men, under the two-fold stimuli of wine and fire, began to sing.

It was an interesting experience to me, for, in times of stress and hardship, the national and racial groups which make up the Legion, and which are largely forgotten under normal conditions, band together for protection or fraternity, as the case may be. This night, the Germans congregated about one fire singing the songs of the Fatherland; from another fire rose the air of an Italian boating song, while from still a third might be heard the strains of a Spanish fandango. I walked about from group to group, talking with the men, drinking an occasional cup of wine with them, and inquiring as to their welfare. As I was about to leave one fire, a voice, coming from the gloom, arrested me.

"Does the Captain speak English?" it said. I replied in the affirmative and received the answer, "Thank God! It's the first time in three years I've had the opportunity to speak my own language."

The voice, it turned out, belonged to an American boy named Hunter who had joined the Legion in search of adventure. I gave him some English newspapers and magazines to read and told him to visit me from time to time when he became homesick for the sound of his native tongue. Later in the same year, at the battle of El Mers (of which more later), Hunter was shot through the leg and invalided home. I have not seen him since.

V

After leaving Azrou, we started to climb, and the weather became definitely cold. We were in hostile country now, and thus were obliged to send out advance, flank, and rear guards to protect the march. No untoward incident occurred, however, to deflect us from the task in hand. Footsore, weary, and dirty we arrived, on the Saturday before Easter, at the bleak mountain post of Timhadit where we halted temporarily, the first portion of our mission accomplished.

Like Azrou, Timhadit is a political post; that is, a post commanded by an army officer on detached service whose duties are to organize the friendly tribesmen, to adjudicate disputes between native craftsmen and the purchasers of their goods, and in general to administer tactfully the French rule, in order that the natives may remain kindly disposed towards the Government. These posts are usually built of whitewashed stone, surrounded by a wall of the same material, and sometimes employ the additional protection of entrenchments and barbed-wire entanglements. They are calculated to withstand a siege, and are impregnable to anything short of artillery fire.

The post-proper of Timhadit is perched upon a dizzy crag, the forward lip of a sort of crater. A desolate, wind-swept spot, but, as it commands the valley below, tactically sound. At the foot of the slope is a supply base, and this location we selected for our encampment. Shortly after our arrival, a native servant reported to the Major with a request from Captain Redier, the post commander, that the officers join him at luncheon. He accepted for us all, and a few moments later we entered the grim gates of the miniature fortress.

Unshaven, tired, and half-frozen as we were, we were amazed at the appearance of Captain Redier, who, perfectly groomed, in glossy boots and unwrinkled uniform, greeted us at the outer door. He looked ready to attend a fashionable race meeting, but, as a matter of fact, we were the first white men he had seen in more than two months. Entering Redier's house, we were further astonished at the contrast it presented to the barren scene without. Here was a veritable salon, richly carpeted, hung with rare old engravings, polished wood gleaming dully from comfortable corners. In this last outpost of a semi-barbarous country, Redier had accomplished the miracle of civilization.

We sat down, in a beautifully appointed dining-room, to a meal that could not have been surpassed at the Ritz. The Major took occasion to compliment our host upon the excellence of his food, but Redier deprecated the really extraordinary meal, saying, "It is unfortunate, gentlemen, that you could not have been here last month, before I lost my cook," and went on to explain the circumstances of his misfortune.

"We are perfectly safe here," he said, "so long as we keep to the post, but, unfortunately, it is necessary for us to go down the mountain to cut firewood, and then we are apt to be attacked by hostile tribesmen. We always go out in strength, but even so we are sometimes compelled to fight our way back. A shot fired in these mountains echoes and re-echoes for miles, and these Berbers flock to the scene of a fight like bees to a honey-pot.

"One morning last month I heard the sound of rifle shots coming from the general direction to which I had dispatched a wood-cutting party. I mounted my horse, and taking with me all my available fighting men, galloped off to the relief. We came up to the party, right enough, to find that it had been ambushed by an immensely superior force and that already we had lost several men, killed or wounded. Within a few moments, we were completely surrounded, and I can tell you that we had the devil's own time in getting back at all.

"Upon our return, I counted noses, only to find that my cook was missing. I inquired among the men as to who had last seen him, and one of them volunteered the information that he had noticed him, just after my own departure, running down the mountainside, rifle in hand, two bandoliers of cartridges slung across his breast. Almost despairing, I sent out several search parties, but they returned without having seen hide or hair of my priceless chef.

"Next morning one of the men reported that he had seen a figure crawling across the snow, far below, at the edge of the woods. I searched the slope with my glasses and finally made out a man—I could not recognize him—apparently wounded and dragging one leg. I sent some men out at once to fetch the fellow in, whoever he was, and they returned within less than an hour with my cook. Shot through the thigh in the previous day's fight, he had been cut off from our party and so was unable to join the withdrawal. In fear of butchering at the hands of the tribesmen, he had dragged himself into the lower branches of a tree where, half-frozen, alternately fainting and conscious, he was obliged to remain for the night, the enemy not having seen fit to leave the woods until dawn. In the morning, then, he tried to win back to the post, and it was during this attempt that we found him. I did all I could for the poor fellow, sending him down to the base and making sure that he received the best of care. The exposure, though, had been too much for him. They amputated his leg, but gangrene had set in and he died a few days later."

He sighed and puffed his cigarette reflectively. "And a damned good cook, too!" said Captain Redier.

CHAPTER TWO

I

WE remained at Timhadit until April 2nd, when we received orders to proceed to Selghert with two companies of the Legion and a half squadron of Spahis. It was the intention of the General Staff to move a quantity of supplies and munitions forward from Timhadit to the advance post of Aghbalou Larbi, from which base, eventually, the spring expedition would operate. While a fairly well-defined road stretched between the posts, it would have been absolutely fatal to send transport through the mountain passes without strong protection.

On the morning of the second, then, we moved out, sending the Spahis ahead as an advance guard, and utilizing our own men as flank and rear guards. During the preceding night it had begun to snow. Morning saw a blizzard in progress, but, after our rest, we pushed forward in good spirits although suffering considerably from the cold.

We had advanced scarcely a kilometre when each step forward became an acute torture. In the passes, the snow had drifted to a depth of eighteen inches or more. A cold wind howled down the narrow gorges, blinding men and animals with stinging particles of ice. The Spahis dismounted and led their horses; our transport mules, heavily laden, began to flounder and fall by the roadside; we called in our flank guards for fear of losing them entirely —oh, a miserable day!

Late in the afternoon, we arrived at Selghert, to find the post fallen to rack and ruin. Except for the four stone walls, in varying states of disrepair, and a leaky shed, there was no shelter available. The storm continuing unabated, we had no choice but to remain where we were, at least for the present. The Major ordered a kitchen set up in the shed; we tethered the mules between the barbed-wire entanglements and the walls; and the men attempted to pitch their shelter tents in the churned-up mud and snow of the quadrangle.

The tent-pitching was decidedly non-successful. Almost as quickly as a tent could be raised, another blew down. Of firewood there was practically none, except for a few wet sticks utilized in the makeshift kitchen where the very floor was a series of pools. Finally, somehow, the cooks managed to serve the evening meal—*la soupe* we call it in the Legion—yet, hungry as we were, we found scant enjoyment in eating it. The shed was filled with dense blue smoke, so overpowering that the cooks were obliged to work in relays. The men lined up and entered the shed in turn, only to rush out again, gasping for breath, to eat cold stew in the full sweep of the storm.

We travel light in the Legion, and so do not encumber ourselves with a proper field kitchen. Each section (about twenty-five men) has its own cook, who draws rations from the non-commissioned officer in charge of supplies, and prepares them over an open fire. In the morning, after réveillé, each man receives a cup of black coffee. At ten-thirty *la soupe*—usually a meat and vegetable stew—is served. At five-thirty *la soupe* appears again, completing the messing for the day. While there is nothing luxurious about this fare, it is, normally, plentiful and wholesome. Company officers, however, do well to keep a careful eye upon the mess, for it is customary—particularly when in garrison—for mess sergeants to sell government supplies in order to purchase liquor.

That night the temperature dropped to six below zero, centigrade (approximately twelve degrees below freezing, Fahrenheit), and there was little sleep for the wet and freezing troops, who had no tents and carried but one blanket apiece. We did not dare to set out a line of outposts, but trusted that the storm would keep the unfriendly natives as quiet as we were obliged to be. Had we been attacked, it would have gone hard with us.

Next morning, we rose—a mere figure of speech—at four, and dispatched a platoon to Aghbalou Larbi for firewood and supplies. The Major decided to ride over also, in order to telephone Headquarters, and asked me to accompany him. We mounted and were floundering towards the road when, suddenly, both Major and pony disappeared in a drift.

I dismounted and managed to extricate him from six feet of snow, the while he cursed roundly in several languages and at least four dialects.

We pushed on again, the storm continuing its fury, and finally reached Aghbalou Larbi and a warm meal. It had taken us four hours to traverse, on horseback, six kilometres! The Major got through to Meknes on the 'phone and asked permission to evacuate Selghert until the weather had grown milder. His request was granted and we started back, our spirits considerably higher.

We reached our troops again in mid-afternoon, anticipating the return of the supply detachment by several hours. Never have I seen a more miserable group of men. The last remnants of morale had disappeared; huddled together in groups, without food, without wine, without courage, they were a sorry illustration of what hardship and privation can accomplish in the short span of a few days. The week before they had been the equals of any troops in the world; now they were a rabble, a collection of human beings, helpless before the fury of the elements.

In even worse condition were the animals. Icicles half a metre long hung from the bellies of the mules; there was no forage; and grazing, in three feet of snow, was impossible. Almost all were frostbitten and several of the poor creatures had died.

The rations finally came up, and the cooks threw together a meal of sorts. Again that night there was no sleep. It was God's own mercy that we were not attacked.

At dawn we started back for Timhadit. I have marched many weary miles over the plains and mountains of Africa, but never have I experienced hardship equal to this. The animals could scarcely be driven forward to break a trail through the drifts. We left behind, to the tender mercies of the natives, all but the most necessary impedimenta, yet the poor creatures were barely able to carry their own weight, let alone what was left of our equipment. Seven of the machine-gun mules died *en route*. We fairly crawled ahead, moving by sheer will power, for there was no strength left in us. The Major and I marched at the rear of the column, forcing the stragglers to keep up. Many of the men threw themselves down to sleep at the roadside, that awful sleep from which there is no awakening, and we were obliged to kick and buffet them to prevent their lapsing into unconsciousness.

Evening again, and the Legion had won through to Timhadit without the loss of a man, although I sincerely believe that the Retreat from Moscow could not have further taxed human strength. At the post all was in readiness; fires lighted in the barracks; a warm meal prepared; and an extra ration of wine for everyone. The Major and I joined Redier for dinner, or, at any rate, I joined him, for, once at table, the Major's head fell forward upon his arms and he slept like one dead. The severe physical strain of the last few days, plus the terrific responsibility of conducting a practically defenceless force through hostile country, had combined to exhaust the man utterly. We put him to bed, and he slept the clock round.

II

The blizzard continued for a week, practically without ceasing. We took an inventory the day after our arrival at Timhadit, and found that 30 per cent. of the troops suffered from frostbite. Two officers and ten men were hospital cases and were sent down to Meknes for treatment. The rest of us spent the time cleaning equipment, cutting and hauling firewood, eating and sleeping a great deal while we had the opportunity.

Equipment cleaning or, as we refer to it, *astiquage*, takes a prominent place in the life of a Légionnaire. Rifles, side-arms and buckles are burnished daily; uniforms must be kept clean and neatly mended; all equipment, in short, goes through a rigid inspection which it ill befalls a man not to pass. This continual washing and polishing, taken in addition to the regular work of a soldier, is, while conducive to discipline, extremely distasteful to the rank and file. Hence, it is customary for many of the men, all those, in fact, who happen to possess a few extra francs, to hire less fortunately situated comrades, at a cost of a few sous a day, to do their *astiquage* for them. Of course, the officers are not supposed to know of this practice; but where life is so hard, it is usual to overlook such small infractions of the rules, particularly when, by so doing, a more equable distribution of wealth may be brought about.

As you will have realized from Captain Redier's story, wood-cutting in the Middle Atlas is more than a simple manual task. During the severe weather, it became necessary for us to replenish our supply several times each week, and, desiring not to lose valuable men, we worked out a scheme which enabled us to carry on the job with comparative safety. Each morning, preparatory to setting out, we placed our machine guns in position and raked the woods with a heavy barrage. It is true that we saw no sign of an enemy during these periods, yet, had snipers been lurking in the underbrush, they would have had an uncomfortable time maintaining their positions. Then, too, the terrific din warned the tribesmen for miles around that we were about to advance in force, and that we were not to be surprised. After the barrage was lifted, the Spahis rode out, to form a complete chain of outguards, and within this armed circle we were able to gather our firewood in peace and quiet. Such elaborate preparations may sound rather ridiculous to the uninitiated reader, yet I venture to predict that even the most intrepid soul, after experiencing a few times the drone of a sniper's bullet close to his head, would go to similar lengths in protecting himself and his men. There is no virtue in being shot from ambush, and no true courage in foolhardiness—particularly when other lives are at stake besides one's own.

III

After we had rested for some weeks, I was sent back to Meknes by motor lorry, to requisition new tentage and supplies to replace those abandoned at Selghert. Although it was still cold, the weather had settled somewhat, and it was thought advisable to get the battalion on to Aghbalou Larbi well before the start of the expedition. Two companies, then, marched to the advance post, accomplishing the trip without event, while a third was sent again to Selghert there to remain temporarily as a protection to transport.

When, some days after the battalion had settled down in its new surroundings, I arrived at Aghbalou Larbi, I found that the Major had ranked me out of the last available downstairs room in the officers' quarters. I set down my kit in the room directly above his and, being tired after the long journey, straightway went to bed. Awakened early the next morning by my orderly, I was amazed and chagrined to find my blankets covered with snow which had sifted through scores of holes in the roof. The floor too was a miniature snowfield which the stove, just kindled, was rapidly causing to melt. Altogether, the situation was rather annoying. I rose, shivering, went below to wash, and directed the orderly to set up a tent over my bed. At least I should sleep dry in the future.

My porous quarters were considered a huge joke at the mess, and no one laughed so loud nor so long as the Major when I related my experience. The next night, however, the tables were turned. Snow fell again, settled upon the steeply pitched fly of my tent, and, melted, gradually, in the heat of the stove. At about midnight I was awakened by the Major's angry bellowing—he had a real talent for profanity—to find that the water had dripped through the floor and soaked his bed. While sympathetic in the extreme, I could not help recalling my superior's amusement at my own plight of the day before. I suggested a compromise, and thenceforth we shared the downstairs room.

IV

Garrison life at Aghbalou Larbi was not unpleasant, especially as we all regarded it as an interlude before the storm. Stationed there, in addition to our own troops, were several companies of the Bataillon d'Afrique and a detachment of Spahis. The men fraternized or quarrelled, as the spirit moved them, and the officers, forming a common mess, managed to while away the long evenings drinking tea and brandy, fighting amiably over bridge games, or singing to the accompaniment of my banjo and a guitar played by young Lieutenant Berger.

The Bataillon d'Afrique, or, as it is vulgarly known to the troops, the *Joyeux*, is the punishment organization which is often, and unfortunately so, confused in the minds of laymen with the Foreign Legion. The " Bat d'Af " is made up of criminals who are given the opportunity to serve in Africa as soldiers in lieu of serving in France as convicts. Here, too, military prisoners and defaulters are sent for discipline, and discipline is what they get. They are given the worst stations, perform the most arduous and distasteful duties, and are subjected to rigorous punishments for the slightest infraction of rules. Most of the officers of the Bat d'Af are Corsicans, picked for their efficiency and severity, and woe betide the soldier who attempts to go contrary to the accepted order of things while under their command. On the other hand, and from my own observations, I do not see that life in the punishment battalions is much worse than in other organizations, always provided, of course, that one is careful not to get oneself into trouble.

The Spahis, on the contrary, are among the finest, and certainly are the most magnificent troops in appearance, that I have ever seen. Officered by Frenchmen, this native cavalry organization prides itself upon its loyalty and devotion to duty. The men are excellent horsemen, uniformly good rifle shots, and are capable of the most amazing feats of endurance. Over their regulation khaki uniforms they wear flowing burnouses of brilliant scarlet, and these, plus turbans worn in place of regulation headgear, combine to give them an air at once distinguished and romantic. In the fighting in the Middle Atlas, and later in the Riff, these splendid troops distinguished themselves upon many occasions, seeming to take a delight in storming the strongest positions, and exhibiting the utmost fierceness in their swift mounted attacks. This eagerness of theirs, in the face of the enemy, is partly due to the fact that they can expect no mercy if captured. The Berbers always kill their prisoners, but for the Spahis they reserve the most exquisite tortures that their cruel and fertile minds have been able to devise.

We remained in this relatively pleasant situation, then, until early in May. One morning, after breakfast, we observed a column crawling slowly up the rough track towards the post and realized that the remainder of our group was about to join us.

Under the command of Colonel Callais of the 6th Moroccan Tirailleurs, came that regiment, several batteries of light artillery, another squadron of Spahis, and the remaining company of our own battalion which had been left behind at Selghert. Soon the quiet garrison took on new life; equipment was overhauled and packed, ammunition served out, and bayonets sharpened. Colonel Callais had arrived with orders to open up the Teghzeft Pass for transport, in order that the expedition, completely supplied, could debouch into the Moulouya plain, from which position—it lay between the Middle and the Grand Atlas ranges—the operations were to be started.

CHAPTER THREE

I

ON May 8th, we got under way, and, advancing in two columns, marched south until we entered the Teghzeft Pass, a narrow defile between two towering peaks of the Middle Atlas. Here we deployed, sending the Spahis ahead, and, after a preparatory barrage, advanced cautiously. We anticipated no trouble but, not caring to lose valuable men in an ambush, took the same precautions we would have observed in an actual attack. No untoward incident marred the movement, and at noon, we arrived at the highest point of the pass, where we found an old, abandoned post. Here, at a height of seven thousand feet, we paused for a short rest and enjoyed a magnificent view. Below us was unfolded the fertile Moulouya plain, dotted here and there with *kasbahs*—the native combination of granary and stronghold; and to the south the Grand Atlas range stretched its jagged fingers into the sky. Then, like the phalanxes of Alexander poised above the Indian plain, we descended but to conquer.

For the next few days the troops put in their time conducting supplies through the pass, while I, on the twelfth, received orders to report to the staff of General Poeymirau at Meknes. I was loath to leave the expedition just at the point when things promised to become interesting, not realizing that, as a staff officer, I should be in a far better position to observe the campaign as a whole than could possibly have been the case had I remained in the line. I made my way back, however, with all possible dispatch, and reported to the General with the best grace I could muster.

The youngest divisional commander in the French Army, General Poeymirau, proved an excellent officer under whom to serve. He was a short, squarely built man, grey-haired, grey-moustached, with a twinkling eye and extraordinarily well-cut uniforms. Indeed, he was the personification of elegance in the military sense—what the British call "swanky"—and quite the reverse, in manner, of the stern type of officer I had learned to expect in the Army of Africa. During the World War, the General had served in France with the Moroccan troops until 1917, when, badly wounded, he had been sent back to Africa to command the Meknes region. His long experience in Morocco had endowed him with uncanny insight into the native mind, a quality which enabled him to lead and administer the colonial troops with unusual success.

Off duty, the General was the most charming of men. He had a wide reputation for running an excellent, though informal, mess. He delighted in visiting the various cafés in company with his juniors. A confirmed bachelor, his entertainments were the highlight of social life in Morocco. In my months of service with him, I never once saw him downhearted or anything but his cheery self. The one drawback to being a member of his staff was that he exposed himself regularly and needlessly to the fire of the enemy and expected us to do the same.

I was appointed liaison officer, a nasty job

in open warfare, entailing constant galloping back and forth between the engaged elements of the command. We remained in Meknes for two days, and, on May 15th, started out by motor for Enjil, where the expedition had concentrated to await our joining them.

During the few days intervening, I improved my time by becoming acquainted with my brother staff officers and in familiarizing myself with my duties. Except for myself, all of the Staff had seen a great deal of African campaigning, and had been chosen because of their special knowledge of native tactics. Major Blanc, the Chief of Staff, had been in Morocco for seventeen years, while Captains De Lattre and Renoir, respectively Operations and Transport officers, had performed similar tours of duty. Captain Le Fèvre, the Intelligence Officer, was perhaps the most valuable of the lot. He had spent years in the Political Section and knew exactly how to handle the Berber kaids, or petty chieftains. He could advise the General, for instance, to avoid fighting a certain tribe in order to engage a second, thus forcing the first and less stubborn group to give us their allegiance through fear of being made to suffer a worse fate than their fiercer allies. He knew the various native dialects and had many underground sources of information. In a country where it is difficult to tell a friend from an enemy, where spies abound in your own camp—selling cigarettes or sweets during the day only to snipe at your tents during the night—such a man is invaluable. If the enemy employed spies, Le Fèvre, in turn, employed others to spy upon them. And, best of all, he knew when to believe a native and when to discount information which, to anyone else, would have appeared authentic.

The mission of our expedition was to penetrate a section known as La Tache de Taza and to reduce the nomadic Berber tribes that infested the region. These tribes, so far as is known, had never been defeated since the dawn of history. Spending their lives alternating between pastoral occupations and robbing their less virile agricultural neighbours, they easily defeated the occasional punitive expeditions sent out by the Sultan. Tall, strong, wiry, and well armed, these men prefer fighting to performing any kind of manual labour.

They know every rock and hiding-place for hundreds of square miles, can live on a handful of dates and a mouthful of water for incredible periods, and do not at all mind being killed provided that, first, they can slaughter a few Christians.

II

On the eighteenth, then, all things being in readiness, we moved out from Enjil, north-east to Lalla Mina. Our intelligence service brought us information that the tribesmen had taken up a strong position on the heights of Bou Arfa, north-west of this point, and General Poeymirau decided to make his reconnaissance, form in battle order, and proceed to the attack on the twentieth. Halting the troops at Lalla Mina, the General went forward with his staff to Souiger, a high point, and from there reconnoitred the enemy's position. We found that he had concentrated in force at Bou Arfa, up the valley, but that his flanks were well protected by high hills, running parallel to our line of advance on both right and left. The General decided to divide our forces, attacking with two columns—one to proceed directly towards the main objective, the second to take care of the flanks. We returned to Lalla Mina, satisfied that we had at least formulated a working plan.

On the morning of the twentieth we moved out before dawn. At about 5 a.m. we established contact with the enemy and were met by a withering rifle fire on our right. This held up our right flank column temporarily, but the General dispatched a battery of seventy-fives from the reserve to help force the Berbers out of a position which, if maintained, might seriously embarrass the central attack. The battery departed at a dead run, careering over the rough trail, gun carriages swinging perilously round sharp curves, gunners clinging to their perches for dear life, while the drivers, swearing cheerfully, urged their teams to a still madder pace. The battery disappeared into the mist almost at once. We feared for the result, but a few minutes later the guns began coughing, slowly at first, then faster as they established the range and began to fire for effect. The General, who had been waiting anxiously, signalled his staff, and we galloped forward to the main attack.

The firing now became general, encircling us on three sides. Our point had reached the base of the enemy position, and a native battalion was ordered to make a frontal attack. It moved forward and was held up some distance from the enemy, when suddenly a heavy fog came down, completely obliterating the result of the movement. The General sent the remainder of the assault group into the line, and ordered me to establish contact with the native battalion.

I spurred forward, guided by the sound of heavy firing, and finally came up to the position. The battalion losses had been terrific; the majority of the French officers were casualties; and ammunition had almost given out. I made my way back to the General, who had, in the meantime, advanced close to the firing line. He ordered me to find the ammunition section, to get hold of the first reserve battalion I could discover, and to bring them both forward to reinforce the line. It was quite impossible, at this time, to see ten feet in any direction. I gave my horse his head, praying that he would not fall, and by sheer luck ran into the ammunition section. My next task was to find a reserve battalion. I galloped about aimlessly for a while, finally to strike my own battalion of the Legion, anxiously awaiting orders. I located Major Büschenschütz and shouted, "Deploy to the right of our first line. Follow me!" He rode up immediately and ordered his troops forward at the double. Again guided by the sound of firing, I led the battalion almost up to the line, halted it there, and pushed ahead to establish exact contact.

As I rode up to the line a breeze sprang up, dissipating the fog in a few seconds. Our native troops were holding on for dear life, while the tribesmen had crawled closer and closer, taking advantage of the low visibility to worm their way from rock to rock, pausing occasionally to fire, and then advancing again.

The lifting fog disclosed a tragic scene. There were no gaps in our line, for corpses cannot move from a position. Here and there a badly wounded soldier turned his gaze to the rear, searching the slope for possible stretcher bearers. Directing the action was a young lieutenant, fresh from St. Cyr. He stood calmly on a little hillock; beside him sat his dog. All this I took in at a glance. As I began to question the lieutenant, a fierce yell drowned my voice. Scarcely twenty yards away a horde of tribesmen had risen, seemingly from out of the ground. They took hasty aim and poured a terrific volley into our decimated ranks. The lieutenant fell, without a word, pierced by a dozen bullets. His dog, badly wounded, ran in circles, howling and snapping at his hurt. As for me, I dived from my horse and hugged the ground.

At the moment, the situation was black enough. The native battalion, terribly cut up and without commissioned officers, could not hold on a great while longer. Without much hope of success, I started forward to take command, expecting the battalion to cut and run at the first sign of an enemy charge. The fierce yells of the tribesmen rose above the sound of firing, and I knew that they were mustering courage to make a rush.

Before they could get started, however, I heard a heavy tramping on the right. There, a few yards away, was my battalion. Grimly, silently, swiftly, the Legion advanced, Major

Büschenschütz at the head. There was no cheering, no waving of banners; just a line of khaki-clad, lean-jawed soldiers setting out to accomplish a professional task. Here and there a man stumbled, pitched forward on his face, to twitch a bit and then lie still. Automatically, the gap was filled, and in less time than it takes to tell it here, the battalion closed with the enemy and got to work with the bayonet.

On our front the firing ceased as the tribesmen attempted to stem the Legion's advance. Encouraged, the native troops ran forward to assist the charge. In a short time the ridge was cleared and we had them on the run.

Elsewhere the battle had progressed more favourably. The tribesmen had seen enough fighting for one day, particularly as their wounded and dead—which they invariably carry to the rear—had thinned out their ranks. They dispersed swiftly, splitting up into small groups, and soon there was left no enemy for us to engage. We occupied the heights, threw up low walls of rock to protect our position, and made camp for the night.

The method of the French in holding conquered territory is simple and effective. It is entirely probable that they learned it from the Roman legions who adopted a similar plan in the conquest of Gaul. The Romans, you will recall, after having defeated a tribe in battle, proceeded to turn artisans, in order to erect a stronghold upon the scene of victory. When, some months later, the Gauls returned in overwhelming numbers to avenge their fallen comrades, they were amazed to find a walled town risen out of the ruins of what had once been a camp site. Pitted against such systematic soldiery, the barbarians were outclassed: they had no choice but, eventually, to submit.

So, in Morocco, we defeat a tribe only to establish a line of stone blockhouses, or outposts, in its territory. These strong points, laid out roughly in sectors and controlled and supplied from a key post, are impregnable to anything but artillery fire. Gradually, by means of fair dealing, we win the natives over. Secure in the protection of the outposts, farms spring up on the fertile slopes. In a few years what was once a wilderness has become a comparatively peaceful agricultural country.

It is not for me to discuss here the pros and

cons of this policy of attrition. Perhaps it is a good thing for the natives to be protected and policed; perhaps not. What concerns us, and what concerns me as a soldier, is that the system works. With a chain of outposts, lightly garrisoned but strategically powerful, it is possible to withdraw the army for service elsewhere. And seldom—except in the war with the Riffi—has an outpost, once established, been taken by the tribesmen.

After Bou Arfa, then, we spent some weeks in building posts and roads. We were joined, during this period, by a second expedition, operating from Fez, and these troops too were pressed into service as engineers. With six hundred men we hewed and blasted a road through the rock of the Reciffa Pass, a Herculean task which, completed in ten days, enabled lorries and heavy transport to penetrate the Moulouya plain through the mountains from Fez.

We established a fortified camp in the plain below Bou Arfa, which grew into quite a town before we had been there for many days. We were surrounded by camp followers of all types: Arab merchants who sold to the troops vile cigarettes and dates of slightly superior quality; native women who were no better than they should have been; café keepers who vended native wines in the shade of skin tents; spies, whom we could not identify; mendicants who lived on our leavings; and thieves who knifed one another in squabbles over their meagre takings. It was all very colourful, and we found it quite a pleasant break in the monotony of our daily lives to walk through the single crooked street of tents, sampling here a glass of wine and there pausing to observe some fakir or juggler in his desperate attempt to entice a few sous from the poverty-stricken soldiery. Pleasant, I say, by day; but if a uniformed man had dared that street after sundown he would never have been heard of again.

On the seventh of June we received orders to move, this time north-east towards Bou Khamouj, where the tribesmen had again concentrated in force. We marched out into the terrific heat—the thermometer had registered one hundred and twenty degrees Fahrenheit at 7 a.m.—covered about twenty-five kilometres during the day, and camped for the night at Ifkain, a *kasbah* situated in the valley some five or six kilometres south of our objective. We remained at Ifkain during the next day while supplies were being rushed up to us by camel caravan. It was a pleasant enough spot, with a stream running through a small fruit orchard, and I remember that I stripped during the afternoon and enjoyed a swim. That night we received orders to attack at 5 a.m.

Leaving the Staff conference that evening, I paused for a moment to gaze in the direction of Bou Khamouj. Our march outposts were engaged in a desultory fire-fight with the enemy scouting parties, and I was curious to know what sort of resistance we should meet in the morning. What was my surprise to note that our camp was ringed, on three sides, by huge bonfires. I later learned that these had been built by the enemy to apprise us that they knew of our plans and to demonstrate that they were ready to cope with our attack.

Promptly at 5 a.m. we formed two columns, deployed, and advanced to a frontal attack on the heights of Bou Khamouj. In the grey dawn, the line of bonfires winked at us cheerfully, seeming to belie the character of the reception which we expected to meet. We advanced rapidly to the banks of a shallow river, immediately below the enemy position, when our left column was attacked on its extreme left flank. My battalion of the Legion, stung by the enemy fire, charged their attackers and routed them at the point of the bayonet. The expedition then negotiated the crossing successfully and took up a temporary position at the foot of the hill.

With the staff I had remained on the near bank of the river. General Poeymirau observed that the attack was being carried out successfully thus far and decided that, despite the hot rifle-fire, we should breakfast here. Our messman came up with a well-laden mule which carried our supplies and tin dishes, and, in order to facilitate matters, I assisted the man in unloading the beast. Suddenly, there was a loud smack! The mule started, then began to groan in a most heartrending fashion. A bullet had struck its jaw, ploughed through the bone and cartilage, and come out the other side. I expected the poor creature to expire at once, but the messman, whistling philosophically the while, unwound his blue woollen sash and wrapped it about the two gaping holes. Then he went on with his unpacking, and the mule, five minutes later, was contentedly munching grass. A wonderful beast!

After a hasty breakfast I was sent by the General to ascertain what held up our left flank, which appeared to be in difficulties. I crossed the river and cantered towards the firing, to arrive just in time to watch a squadron of Spahis carrying out a magnificent bit of manœuvring. They had dismounted to fight on foot a few minutes previous to my arrival, and had successfully beaten off an attack when a second group of natives charged our infantry several hundred yards ahead. Vaulting into their saddles the Spahis were off at a headlong gallop almost before I could believe my eyes. Halfway to the scene of the new trouble their captain's horse was shot from under him and he was catapulted to the ground some yards ahead. Unhurt, however, he signalled them to go on. They galloped as close to the enemy as the huge rocks which barred their way permitted, again dismounted, and, not pausing for an instant, charged the tribesmen who had, for some minutes past, been giving the native infantry considerable trouble.

In the meantime, the frontal attack had progressed with fair success. The native position, on the "military crest"—slightly forward of the actual crest—of a long ridge was exposed to an artillery drum-fire, augmented by machine-guns and rifles. We could see that it was only a matter of an hour or so before they would be compelled to abandon their line. To the left, however, of their main position was a steep wooded hill, rising some three or four hundred feet above the normal terrain. It seemed to the General unusual that the natives should not have occupied this commanding height, yet all through the battle it had remained silent—aloof and austere above the petty bickerings of men. Silent or no, the General smelled a rat and, to be on the safe side, dispatched a native battalion to investigate. They swung swiftly forward, deployed, and disappeared among the cedar trunks.

For fifteen or twenty minutes, nothing unusual occurred. Then, with a startling crash, the hidden Berber riflemen opened up on their attackers. Due to the thickly wooded terrain they had been able to out-manœuvre our troops without giving themselves away. They rained bullets from three sides, killing or wounding the French officers at the outset and completely ruining the morale of the advancing force.

Without officers, the native troops degenerated into a bewildered herd. Whichever way they turned they were met by rifle-fire. Liaison between elements was impossible in the forest; men dropped on all sides stricken by the unseen steel-jacketed hail; the attack became a retreat, a rout, a shambles. The ambush was a complete success.

All this, of course, we learned later. Now, we searched the slopes with our glasses, realizing from the sound of heavy firing that a hot fight was in progress. After a time, our soldiers began to drift back from the forest, singly at first, then in couples, in small groups herded together with the instinct—of dubious value in such a contingency—for safety. Soon they started running towards us, throwing down their arms to facilitate progress, completely terror-stricken. The retreat had become a catastrophe. We found afterwards that they had lost seventy killed and two hundred and twenty-eight wounded.

While all this had been happening, our main attacking force had advanced with the bayonet and cleared the main ridge. The tribesmen melted away before our charge, carrying with them their wounded and most of their dead. Dissatisfied, however, with our fiasco on the left, particularly as the still-occupied hill commanded our own position, General Poeymirau dispatched a battalion of the Legion to the assault.

Now the Legion, unlike other "crack" organizations of which I have heard tales, takes its fighting with befitting seriousness. The severe contrasts of the Moroccan climate, alone, are enough to prevent unseemly levity, and it is not very amusing to be shot at from ambush by an enemy with whom it is next to impossible to come to grips. Advancing in thin, far-flung lines, through retarding sand, over sun-baked rocks, losing here an officer, there a man, it is only too heartbreakingly often that the Legion comes up, finally—with nothing. And so the Étrangères are a little grim in setting about their business. They are, in the most literal sense, "professionals." For them there is no glory: they do not suffer and fight and die *pour la patrie.* They are the lost sheep; but their hearts are the hearts of lions.

So the battalion entered the wood, silent and sure, calm in the knowledge that no native force had ever stood up before the Legion's direct assault. There had been a lull in the firing, the Berbers, probably, having paused to loot our dead. Now it rose again to fiercer heights as the tribesmen strove desperately to stem the advance. We could see nothing, but soon a steady rataplan announced to us that our men had halted to open a fire-fight. There was no cheering—even the Moors forgot to yell—yet we detected the progress of our troops in the gradual decrease of enemy fire. A few minutes later, the General sent me forward to ascertain the result. I rode up the hill to find the Legion in possession.

Our losses, though, had again been heavy, and it was thought unadvisable to attempt to hold on through the night. Having proved to the enemy that we could dislodge them at will, we caused the battalion to withdraw in order to join us on the main ridge, where we worked frantically to prepare a fortified camp before darkness should set in.

The stony surface prevented our digging trenches, so we threw up low walls of rock for our protection. While we worked, the tribesmen, worming their way from one bit of cover to another, drew once more within easy rifle-shot. We could not see them, and nothing short of a direct assault could force them out. Soon they had ringed the camp, concentrating particularly upon the abandoned hilltop which overlooked us, and from these carefully concealed positions they poured a nerve-racking harassing fire into our tents.

There was no sleep for us that night. Our own machine-guns kept up a continuous retaliatory fire which, really, was more annoying to the exhausted troops than the occasional drone of an enemy bullet. True, we had severe casualties before morning; but the Berbers are not expert rifle-shots and, luckily for us all, most of their fire went high, either whizzing harmlessly over the camp or ripping through tent-tops with exasperating though seldom lethal effect. We realized then that we should have held the overhanging hill, at all costs, and that we should have no respite from the constant sniping until we had retaken it.

The next day—the eleventh—was devoted to rest; that is to say, all hands worked frantically on the fortifications and at bringing up munitions. Constant firing kept our nerves on edge, and the General decided to take the hill the following morning at dawn. Three battalions were assigned to the task, my own battalion of the Legion taking the centre section, and I was sent with the assault group as Staff representative.

At 4.30 a.m., we assembled in the mist, preserving the greatest possible silence, allowing the men neither to talk nor to smoke. A slight rattling at the whispered command to fix bayonets could scarcely be heard a dozen yards away. We depended upon the surprise effect of our attack to disconcert the enemy, and hoped thus to avoid unnecessary casualties. I think that we all felt a bit jumpy that morning—I know that I did—for, despite all our elaborate precautions, we felt that the Berbers would be ready for our advance. Four-thirty a.m., while it may be a very good hour for a surprise attack, is, nevertheless, an exceedingly bad hour for the morale of men who are about to face fire.

The advance began auspiciously, however, and we were soon making the best of our way up the wooded slopes. Sniping had ceased for an hour or two (I assume that even Moors must sleep occasionally), and there was little indication that this was anything more than a practice march or wood-cutting expedition. We hoped to get near enough to the enemy to close with him, saving the cost of a lengthy rifle and machine-gun duel, and, for once, we were successful in eluding his habitually watchful eye.

Our forward elements were within a hundred yards of the summit before the enemy learned of our presence. Then they started firing hysterically, doing no damage at all, and we assaulted the crest without stopping to shoot. Another minute and we were at their stone breastworks, which the Légionnaires leapt to perform fearful execution with the bayonet. The battalions on the right and the left closed in rapidly, employing hand grenades with which they blasted out such stubborn groups as refused to surrender or retire. The assault was a complete success, and after five or six minutes of hand-to-hand work, we had the tribesmen on the run. Once they broke, the retreat became a panic. They tore down the reverse slope of the hill and, entering the plain, were caught by our artillery, which fired rapidly and with great accuracy from positions on the main ridge. The Spahis rode fiercely to the pursuit but were soon recalled by the General, who had no intention of allowing them to be carried away by our success to such an extent that they would venture too far afield from the base.

It might have been expected, from our victory, that the power of the tribesmen was broken; that they would have had, by now, enough of such disastrous campaigning. Unfortunately for us, these fierce mountaineers do not fight according to our civilized rules and standards. When they smell defeat in the wind, they usually—except in a few isolated instances—make a rapid withdrawal, scattering in a dozen directions as soon as they have got beyond rifle range. They do not consider these tactics a disgrace; nor, in fact, does it ever occur to them that they have suffered a defeat. Fighting they love; but they take it casually, returning to their homes when the whim strikes them, only to come again to harass us upon another more auspicious occasion. This system of making war is, of course, ideally suited to the nature and capabilities of the Berber. In familiar country, one tribesman is the equal of four or five European-trained soldiers, for the simple reason that he is not bothered for supplies and is not obliged to operate from an advanced base. His system is primitive, inexpensive, and effective—he learns all that is necessary for him to know, by word of mouth; if he is hungry, he returns home to eat; if he is tired, to sleep.

And, knowing all this, we were not surprised, that night, when rifle-fire started again. Our next task was to establish a post system in the Bou Khamouj sector. We received the fire as our due, replied to it with equanimity, and looked forward to the day when we should get another opportunity to come to grips with these annoying fellows who stung us as we laboured.

CHAPTER FOUR

I

THE work at Bou Khamouj kept us employed until the twenty-first of June. During that period, we were almost continuously under fire, a circumstance made the more annoying because of our inability to retaliate. The great necessity for the tribesmen is to possess themselves of rifles and ammunition, and to this end they ambushed our smaller working parties daily, rising from behind rocks to shoot at short range, then closing in with knives to dispatch the wounded and rob them of arms and ammunition. It was all accomplished in a trice, and then they were off again among the rocks—beyond punishment.

The rifle stealing became so bad that we actually lost arms out of the tents at night.

During the day, the camp followers—many of whom were undoubtedly our enemies—hung about our guard lines, selling the usual cigarettes and dates. After sundown, they took to the hills and started sniping again. Then, occasionally, two or three of them would sneak past a sentry—their ability to move noiselessly is uncanny—enter a tent, knife the sleeping soldiers, and steal their arms. Finally, we were obliged to devise a system whereby each squad wrapped its weapons in a tarpaulin and buried them in a trench before retiring. The trench was then filled loosely with earth, and the men lay across it.

The native women, too, took up positions around the camp after sundown. They were —if it is possible—more bloodthirsty than the men, making the night hideous with their screams, curses, and threats of vengeance. A favourite diversion with them is to shout at our native troops, calling to them to desert the hated *Roumis*, and threatening them with all sorts of ingenious tortures if they fail to obey. Their cries do no serious damage, as the native troops are habitually loyal. But it is a fact that the women are permitted to torture all prisoners and that they visit battlefields after dark to perform the same service upon any wounded men whom we may have been careless enough to leave behind.

It is the Berber practice first to torture and then to kill all prisoners or wounded who fall into their hands, although now and again a man has been let off with castration. Our own men, of course, are fully cognizant of what fate awaits them if, perchance, they are left alive upon the field; and it is seldom—except through surprise—that a man allows himself to be taken. There is always, as Rudyard Kipling advised the young British soldier, a final cartridge in reserve to cheat the torturers.

The French have been often accused—and, I think, with some injustice—of needless butchery during the course of these native wars. I had imagined that, since the World War, most people were aware that battles differ somewhat from sporting events, but apparently such is not the case. In any event, I assure my readers that it is next to impossible to make a prisoner of a Berber. I have seen more than one misguided Samaritan attempt to extend aid to wounded tribesmen only to be stabbed or shot for his pains.

Everyone knows, of course, that the Musulman believes the killing of a Christian to be a deed peculiarly acceptable in the sight of Allah; that each Christian butchered means another houri in Paradise. Naturally, then, the wounded or dying tribesman has everything to gain in doing away with a few additional Frenchmen, and nothing to lose. If the wounded man is able to aim, he continues to fire until his ammunition is exhausted, or until he is killed. If one bends over to offer him water, or other aid, he has recourse to his long knife. I have seen one of my own men stabbed in this manner, by a native so sorely wounded that the effort of driving home the knife killed him. We do not, then, make a practice of taking prisoners or of aiding the wounded, unless we are certain that they are unarmed. I believe that any army, in the circumstances, would comport itself similarly.

We had completed our work, as I said, by the twenty-first. Next morning, we broke camp at dawn—to the considerable delight of the taunting tribesmen—and marched north-west towards Athea.

Again it was very hot, so hot that men dropped like flies along the line of march. At midday we were forced to halt for four hours, it being deemed impossible to push on farther while the sun beat down so mercilessly. We wished, if possible, to get within striking distance of the town of El Mers—the Berber stronghold—ere night had set in, for the effort of building a fortified camp, *en route*, only to abandon it next morning, was a task to be avoided. Thus we marched out at a brisk pace, despite the still powerful sun, and came up to our objective at about eight o'clock in the evening.

During the last hour of our march, clouds had been gathering, and now lightning played fitfully over the surrounding peaks, while thunder rolled down the valleys, echoing and re-echoing like the artillery of hell. Suddenly, the storm broke above us as we toiled to pitch our tents in the fast-increasing darkness. In an instant, all was pandemonium. The cloud-burst, it seemed, had deliberately picked us for its victims, and before its fury had been spent, eight members of a native battalion had been killed by lightning.

As quickly as it had struck us, the storm disappeared, leaving a tired, wet, and dispirited force in its wake. The incident of the lightning had spread some disaffection among the native troops, who superstitiously attributed their comrades' death to the fury of Allah who, according to their reasoning, had visited a punishment upon them because of their part in the campaign. On the eve of a battle, such a blow to the morale is no trifle, and it was a worried group of officers who gathered later, during the evening, to discuss plans of attack for the morrow.

The village of El Mers, situated at the extreme northern end of a narrow valley, surrounded on three sides by steep slopes, was the central stronghold of all the tribes in this section of the Middle Atlas. We knew that the battle for the possession of the town would be the high point of our campaign, and that, once it was taken, the backbone of the native resistance would have been broken. Not caring, then, to fail in this most important attack —even temporarily—the General decided against our resting on the morrow, figuring that each additional hour of delay would enable the tribesmen to reinforce their positions.

Good soldiers, of course, make a habit of grumbling. And the Legion grumbles loudest of all when nothing very serious has happened. Yet to-night, when they were informed that they were to lead the attack next morning, the Légionnaires wasted no time in talking but set philosophically about putting their equipment into the best possible condition. Perhaps they comported themselves with such docility because of their weariness, perhaps because rumours had reached them of anticipated trouble with some of our Moroccan battalions. At any rate, they soon settled themselves to snatch what sleep they could, leaving the other elements of our force to follow their example or not, as they saw fit.

We started out at dawn, advancing, as usual, in two groups, with the intention of clearing the flanking hills, thus to converge upon the village when all outlying bodies of tribesmen had been swept before us. On the left the Spahis, who led off, met with almost immediate opposition. Their route of advance was through a lush country, fat pasture lands alternating with fields of waving grain which grew almost shoulder high, and the enemy showed that they meant to sell dearly the fruits of their toil. It is a pity, of course, to be obliged to trample crops underfoot, yet the Spahis had no choice in the matter, fearing that the tribesmen lurked among these same cornstalks—and with good reason.

They started out walking their horses, which seemed to sink almost out of sight as they entered a cornfield, but increased the gait to a brisk trot as the enemy opened fire. The range, as yet, was fairly long, so that the brave spectacle of these red-burnoused horsemen advancing into action was but occasionally marred by a casualty. Before long, however, the distance separating them from the Berbers had decreased appreciably, man after man was seen to pitch from his saddle, riderless horses began galloping here and there to add to the confusion, and we observed—with the aid of our glasses—that the officers were giving the signal to charge.

Orders were given to the infantry to follow

up the Spahi attack, and the left battalions advanced at the double. They entered the action a few minutes later, in time to take advantage of the shock inflicted by the cavalry, but not soon enough to save the horsemen from severe punishment. Shaken by the combined assault, the tribesmen gave way rather easily, and the advance upon the town from this sector progressed more smoothly than we had dared hope. I found, however, before leaving for the right flank, that every commissioned officer in the Spahi squadrons had been either killed or wounded.

At about this time it became apparent that something serious was taking place on the right, and I was dispatched immediately to locate the trouble. Dismounting well behind the firing line, I made my way forward, taking what advantage I could of the scanty cover, and finally reached one of the Legion battalions which had been pinned to the ground on the crest of a low hill. I realized at once that the situation was a nasty one. Owing to the nature of the terrain the battalion could neither advance nor retreat without suffering disproportionate casualties, while to remain on the hill was scarcely preferable, as the enemy riflemen had perfect observation from their own well-protected position on higher ground. I looked about for the battalion commander and found him trying to get a machine-gun set up. I wormed my way along the ground towards him but, before I could get within conversational range, he had been killed.

Obviously the solution of our problem was to blast the enemy out from behind his stone breastworks, and to this end I sent back three runners by different routes with instructions to bring up a battery of mountain artillery. One of the men was wounded before he had covered fifty yards, but the other two disappeared safely over the ridge to our rear, and I breathed more freely.

The machine gunners finally got their weapon mounted (they had been obliged to work from a prone position, owing to the lack of cover) and a young corporal sat up to take aim. He had scarcely raised his body from the ground before he toppled over, fairly riddled with bullets. Nothing daunted, a second member of the gun team tried his luck, only to meet with the same experience before he had succeeded in getting off a single shot. The tribesmen had the position spotted and did not mean to allow that gun to go into action.

By this time I had reached a point alongside and slightly to the rear of the gun. I saw the futility of expending more lives in attempting to fire from there—although the surviving members of the team were beside themselves with rage and quite willing to take the chance—and ordered the men to crawl forward, grasp the legs of the tripod, and drag the gun to the rear, from which point it could be carried to a slightly more protected position, a few yards to the right. This they succeeded in doing without further casualties, and we were soon ready to make another attempt.

This time I called for a volunteer to fire the gun and, as each member of the squad applied for the job, at last picked a man myself, an old Légionnaire who could be trusted to take every advantage of the almost non-existent cover. He reached the gun and raised his body slowly, almost imperceptibly, in order to avoid attracting the enemy's attention by any sudden movement. He must have had an iron grip upon his nerves. It seemed, this time, as if we were going to succeed. The gunner was in position. He raised the sight-leaf and adjusted his aim. In a moment, now, we should hear the first burst, the staccato ta-ta-ta-ta-ta that would increase our fire-power by fifty rifles. Then they got him. . . .

It was, to say the least, disheartening. One active machine-gun would have helped the battalion enormously. The moral effect, alone, of an automatic weapon is tremendous, not to speak of the actual damage it can inflict upon an enemy force. I turned again to the thinned-out gun team and selected a young Dane to make the attempt. He grinned at me cheerfully, and said: "Well, here goes little Denmark." I felt rather that way about it myself, and was half inclined to abandon the whole business. The boy moved up at once, however, and before we could restrain him, rose to his full height and walked calmly towards the gun, just as if there had not been at least a score of riflemen trying their level best to do him in. Naturally, we expected him to last about half a minute, but, as he sat down to take the firing position, a shell burst over the enemy breastworks, followed by another, and another in quick succession. The mountain guns had come up, and unnoticed by us, gone into action from the ridge to our rear.

Then the machine-gun opened up and forced the Berber heads down. On our left, a second gun got into action; the mountain artillery, firing shrapnel, placed their shells with a precision that was a real pleasure to observe; the battalion ceased firing and waited for the order to charge.

The guns, though, had accomplished the job. When, after a twenty-minute barrage, we advanced, it was only to find the Berber positions deserted and the Berber forces carefully re-entrenched a thousand yards ahead, in the outskirts of El Mers. We halted, after having gone ahead a few hundred yards, in the shelter of a steep bank, sent back for stretcher-bearers to take care of the wounded, and furnished details from each platoon to replenish the supply of ammunition. Although it was now but ten o'clock in the morning, we had already seen a hard day's fighting.

My task of the moment accomplished, I returned to the Staff and awaited further orders. I found that both of our columns were within striking distance of El Mers, and that it was the General's plan to push home the attack as soon as he had got all his available artillery and machine-guns into position and ready to fire for effect. Now, I learned further, was an excellent moment at which to partake of luncheon.

That was one of the amazing characteristics of General Poeymirau. He could remain awake all night planning an attack, go breakfastless in the morning, ride for miles—here directing the battle as a general officer should, and there leading a platoon in person; all these things he could and did do. But never, in any circumstances, would the General forgo his luncheon. I have lunched with him under all kinds of conditions; in rain and mud and snow; in battle, while directing under fire; and in the best hotels and restaurants Morocco affords. And always, no matter what dire things were happening, he was equally affable, equally courteous. A man who lived, almost continually, at high pressure (who had lived that way for thirty-odd years), I really believe that the General owed his health, possibly his life, to this ability to relax completely during his meals.

I do not mean to imply by this that he was a trencherman, in the accepted sense. Rather a gourmet than a gourmand, he had early learned a lesson well known to all Latins: that one cannot trifle with one's stomach with any degree of safety, and that to live as gracefully as possible, in whatever circumstances into which one may be thrown, is an important part of life.

We lunched, then, on a delectable chicken stew, provided by the Staff cook, washed down with some remarkable Burgundy supplied by the General. The troops, too, considering the circumstances, fared well, for the cooks had been left behind at the previous night's camp to prepare a hot meal. This was brought forward during the lull in the battle, and successive details of men were relieved from the firing line for a long enough period in which to make a decent luncheon. And so it was with something approaching equanimity that we faced the prospect of a hard afternoon's fighting, after our strenuous efforts of the morning.

The troops remained in their positions, roughly encircling El Mers, during the heat of the afternoon, while our artillery poured high explosive into the town. Rifle and machine-gun fire became general, mounting in volume as the day grew shorter. On the outskirts of the town, some two hundred yards forward of the main group of houses, stood a *kasbah* which had been turned into a fortress, and it became apparent that this sturdy, low-lying structure was the Berber's key position which would have to be taken before we could carry the town proper. The enemy had mounted several machine-guns in the *kasbah*, with which they kept up a lively fire. On either side of the building they had entrenched themselves, the rough earthworks diverging slightly like the barbs of a broad spearhead. It is always difficult to estimate their numbers, but I should say that this particular position was held by about a thousand determined men.

At about three o'clock we began a general advance, sending three battalions of the Foreign Legion against the *kasbah* as assault troops, and pushing ahead with the remainder of our forces, except for a small reserve, on either flank. It was a fairly dangerous move to make, for, had the Legion failed to take its objective, our right and left flanks would have lost contact, standing a very fair chance of being badly cut up. The tribesmen, it must be remembered, stood in no particular awe of us, despite their several reverses at our hands. These men, doubtless, had been near defeat many times previously, yet always they had been ultimately successful. It is difficult to intimidate a free people, who have maintained their autonomy through countless centuries of incessant warfare. Their morale, consequently, remained unimpaired and, in their minds at least, there was no doubt of the final outcome.

It was my task to remain with the central attacking force, maintaining contact with the supply sections and reserve, so that it was not my lot to observe the actual taking of El Mers. The two flanking parties made fairly rapid progress at first, but were held up outside the town. Then the Legion advanced on the *kasbah*, and I was kept occupied for the remainder of the afternoon.

After a heavy preparatory barrage—which

did not seem to inconvenience the enemy in the slightest—we assaulted the trenches with one battalion. The terrain was excellent so far as movement was concerned, yet its very simplicity proved a great hindrance, for the machine-guns in the enemy fortress swept our men away like flies. Three times the battalion charged, only to break, in each instance, at the centre, as the fire from the *kasbah* thinned out the ranks After sustaining heavy losses, the attackers retired in good order to give a fresh force an opportunity for glory.

Of course, the other battalions kept up a heavy covering fire as long as possible, suspending it only when each attack went home. I remained with them, and soon became so interested in what was going on before me that I quite forgot that we too were getting our fair share of casualties. Standing above a squad of riflemen, who pumped bullets towards the enemy like so many automata, I searched the terrain with my glasses, watching the operation unfolding before me as if it were some marionette show on a gigantic scale. Suddenly, I felt a sharp blow on my left thigh. I knew that I had been hit, and wondered that I did not fall. I looked at my leg and was surprised to find it bloodless and apparently intact. Then I noticed a soldier who lay at my feet, grinning up at me. "Sit down, Captain!" he said, "or you'll be killed!" He had struck me with his rifle-stock to attract my attention, and to remind me that it is foolish to expose oneself unnecessarily.

It was decided now to send two comparatively fresh battalions against the trenches to the right and left of the *kasbah*. We felt that, if we could take these, and thus turn both flanks inward, the fortress itself could be surrounded and so forced to surrender. We calculated correctly enough, so far as the tactics of the thing were concerned, but we had figured, as things turned out, without taking the fanatical Moslem mind into consideration.

That was a beautiful assault. We advanced slowly, in small groups, saving our breath for the bayonet work. A perfect fury of fire met us as the enemy realized our intention, and the line staggered for a moment, shook itself, and then went on. Inevitably as fate itself, the Legion drew closer. Men were dropping in scores; it seemed as if the distance to the trenches would never diminish. Yet, suddenly, we were there. I don't believe I actually heard anything, but it seemed to me that there was a sort of a grunt, a guttural, satisfied sound. Then, setting itself, the Legion rushed!

It was bloody work. The tribesmen, cut off from any possible assistance, flatly refused to surrender. Throwing their rifles down, they drew their long knives, and though they were no match for the needle-bayonets of the Légionnaires, sold their lives as dearly as possible.

The *kasbah* simply poured fire into the trenches, killing and wounding friend and foe alike. The inmates knew that they were doomed; knew that not a man could win free; and conducted themselves with the reckless bravery of the old northern Berserkers.

The butchery in the trenches continued for some time, each man fighting with fierce desperation until wounded in a vital spot or killed. After a while, a few squads were able to detach themselves from the shambles in order to rally under a lieutenant who had been delegated beforehand to make the final assault upon the *kasbah*. These men, some twenty in all, laid their rifles down, slung sacks of hand grenades about their necks, and crouched like sprinters awaiting the gun. At a given signal, they sprang towards the *kasbah*, those who survived the first volley covering the inconsiderable distance in a few seconds. These men, pulling the pins with their teeth, flattened themselves against the walls and hurled grenade after grenade through windows and loopholes. After a short time, they ceased operations, and there was no further demonstration from the defenders—for good reason, they having been killed to the last man.

With the storming of the *kasbah* the backbone of the defence crumbled. Those of the enemy who retained any stomach for fighting withdrew from the village to a high ridge some twenty kilometres to the north, and the army, despite its fatigue and the comparative lateness of the hour, was ordered to push on. We did not mean to allow them to consolidate again. Just before darkness closed down we came to the ridge. We were impatient of further delay, so that without bothering to prepare a formal plan of attack, we rushed and took the place after a short sharp fight.

Camp was pitched on the scene of this final struggle.

El Mers, really, was the high point of the campaign. There were other battles, it is true, but these were lesser affairs involving comparatively small forces. Our great trouble now was with snipers, and these pests redoubled their efforts in attempting to exact revenge for their crushing defeat. That night, alone, forty men were killed or wounded in the Staff camp, and God knows how many others were struck while attempting to sleep in the regimental encampments.

Luckily for us, the snipers had difficulty in keeping their aim sufficiently low to do the amount of harm of which they were actually capable. At that, my messman was killed across the table as he attempted to serve me *la soupe*.

At the foot of the ridge, a casualty clearing station had been established. I strolled in that direction, after a somewhat less than satisfactory dinner, intending to look up any of my own men who had been wounded and who might wish for some small assistance, or at least be glad to know that someone was interested in their welfare.

There, huddled at the base of an escarpment, was a group of hastily erected marquees, surrounded on three sides by a brown sea of litters, white-spotted with anguished faces. One of the tents had been utilized as an operating theatre, for the more urgent cases, while others were used as dressing stations. There was, as yet, no means of bringing lorries up to this point, so that the wounded were evacuated by mule transport.

I threaded my way between the litters, pausing here and there to light and bestow a cigarette. A voice hailed from the gloom, "Oh, Captain!" and I changed my direction slightly to come upon Hunter, the American lad, drilled through the thigh but apparently in the best of spirits. I gave him a packet of cigarettes and stopped to chat for a few moments. He told me that he had caught a nasty wound and that he was glad of it, for it would incapacitate him for further service. I agreed that even a painful injury may have its compensations, and went on, never to see him again. Later I learned that he had been invalided from the service and returned to the United States.

Operations continued for three or four days, but, as I have said, the spirit of the natives had been broken. We again set about erecting outposts and building roads and bridges capable of bearing motor traffic, while the few tribes who remained hostile contented themselves with sniping and an occasional ambush. When a pitched battle became necessary, it was usually on a comparatively small scale, and a few battalions were detached, in each of several instances, to perform the fighting.

II

Now that the campaign had been practically concluded, I became heartily bored with soldiering in this comparative wilderness. (It had never occurred to me to be fed up while in the midst of an exciting campaign, but road-building affords one plenty of time for thinking.)

There was little time for excessive boredom, however, for now rumours began to trickle in from the mountains, rumours that the tribesmen had been reinforced, that they were taking heart again, and that we should soon be compelled to renew the campaign. Personally, I found this hard to believe, for I had not yet been sufficiently long in Morocco to absorb the native conception of warfare. A crushing defeat, it seemed logical to me, meant speedy surrender. I could not imagine that the tribesmen would be foolish enough to take up arms again after the terrific drubbing they had received at El Mers. I remarked as much to my brother officers, who replied that, so far as logic went, they were with me, but that the Berber had never been noted as, nor was he now, a logician.

Sure enough, after remaining in the vicinity of El Mers for some days, we received orders to move and once again started out to subdue these apparently unsubduable barbarians.

On the first night of our march, unless my memory fails me, we halted in the almost dry bed of the Leghina River. Inasmuch as we had been working, for days, almost beyond human endurance, a general order was issued bearing the welcome news that we were to remain at the halting place for twenty-four hours in order to give the men an opportunity to rest and the animals a chance to fatten a bit on the lush grass which grew close to the barely trickling stream. The army pitched camp on the river bank, leaving the mules tethered in groups of ten, watched over by a few herd-guards, munching away peacefully at the unfamiliar grass of the river bed.

The Spahis had camped on a little hill adjacent to the stream, and at noon the following day I walked over to visit them, finding myself well repaid for my short journey with a pressing invitation to remain for luncheon. Their food, of course, was much the same as mine, but everyone's mess seems superior to one's own after a few weeks of monotonous fare. At any rate, there I stayed, talking pleasantly with the lieutenant in charge as we shared a bottle of wine and idly watched the activity in the stream bed below.

At about one o'clock, storm clouds gathered, thunder rolled ominously, and incandescent forks of lightning appeared against an almost sable sky. The Spahi watched the clouds uneasily, dispatched his orderly with instructions to see that the horses were securely tied, and remarked anxiously upon the unstrategic position of the mules. The storm blew over us and broke in the mountains far above. We thought no more about it.

Perhaps a quarter of an hour later we heard a dull roaring sound which grew louder even as we first took notice of it. "The river bed!" said the Spahi in alarm. We sprang to our feet to warn the mule guards, but it was too late. Advancing with the speed of doom itself was a fifteen-foot wall of water, a mud-brown torrent carrying destruction in its wake.

Most of the men and many of the mules were able to scramble to safety. Others, however, who delayed a moment too long, were swept away on the crest of the flood never to be seen again. It was a horrible experience for me; worse, almost, than the slaughter of a pitched battle. There I stood, absolutely helpless, without a chance of lending aid to any one, while poor devils were carried down-stream, kicking and lunging until struck, perhaps, by a floating tree, or tumbling head over heels in the swirling rapids. One man, at least, was able to save himself. Swept towards a small island in the middle of the stream, he grasped the extended branch of a small tree and drew himself up slowly as the hungry waters licked about his feet and legs. Later, when the worst of the flood was over, we were able to rescue him with lariats. In all we lost five men and twenty mules, all due to the carelessness of officers who, knowing perfectly well that such storms were of common occurrence, did not bother to post guards to sound the warning.

We marched and counter-marched, after the seemingly senseless manner of armies, until July 13th, without once more coming to grips with anything more tangible than heat and insects. Then we were ordered back to the base camp from which we had launched the attack upon El Mers. There, on July 15th, we met an imposing delegation of Staff officers from the garrisons, who had come out especially to award decorations to the combatant troops. We passed in review; speeches were made, compliments passed, and, together with many others more worthy of the honour, I received the Croix de Guerre.

We moved again, after the festivities, and

upon the seventeenth camped on the outskirts of the hamlet of Atier. At about ten o'clock that night, after everyone had turned in, rifle-fire broke out, ringing the encampment, but heaviest from the north-west. At this point, the tribesmen, who had crept up under cover of darkness, could not have been more than two hundred yards distant from our encampment, and, as they were in some force, our tents were soon riddled. The discipline of our force was, of course, very high, and the men routed themselves out at once to line up, in good order, in the company streets. (Let me say here that none but well-trained troops are capable of calmness in such trying circumstances.) We pushed out, shortly, and formed a firing line outside the encampment, yet it was all we could do to dislodge the tribesmen within two hours. Just before the enemy withdrew, the gallant Major Büschenschütz, who had been indefatigable in directing our counter-attack, received a Mauser bullet through the chest. One lung was pierced and, as there was no field hospital within miles, we despaired of his life. I called for volunteers among the men of our battalion, and as the entire personnel responded, finally picked twenty of them to carry him to the rear. While four men supported the Major on a litter, the remainder of the force acted as advance, flank, and rear guards. They carried him back twelve miles in a trifle more than two hours and a half, saving his life.

During the engagement, my baggage mule was killed, and my cook served me with mule steaks—which were not at all bad—for the next forty-eight hours.

We advanced, the next morning, to the right of Bou Khamouj and there engaged the enemy once more. We attacked him on the nineteenth with some measure of success and, after resting for a day, pushed him out of his positions on the twenty-first.

After this we remained in camp until August 11th, drawing new arms and equipment from the supply train and refurbishing ourselves generally. The eleventh found us again on the march, but most of the native opposition had come to an end and we proceeded northeast to Jebel Illan without event. Near there we consolidated for the winter, and with the exception of a minor engagement at Ait Bessar

—fought on September 3rd—the campaign was brought to a definite close.

Towards the middle of October, the rains began and the troops returned to their regular barracks in the several garrison towns, leaving detachments behind to hold the newly erected outpost line—a dreary prospect.

In the course of the campaign we had lost, in killed, about a hundred officers and three thousand men. The wounded and other casualties were proportionately numerous. La Tache de Taza—the bugbear of many a Sultan—had been considerably reduced; the tribesmen had learned a harsh lesson; and, during the winter, one after another of the Kaids reported to the military governor with his tribe's formal submission. Even now, of course, the locality is unsuitable for pleasure trips, but it will not be much longer before the rich natural resources of the Middle Atlas can be developed.

PART II

CHAPTER ONE

ON the eleventh of November, 1923—the anniversary of Armistice Day—the units that had taken part in the expedition into La Tache de Taza were massed in the great square at Meknes for a final review by General Poeymirau. I had remained a member of the Staff, and so, at 8 a.m., came down with the reviewing party. The General congratulated his veterans and decorated a number of officers and men; the massed bands struck up the March of the Legion, and the troops swung into column for the last time.

It was, to a soldier's eyes, a magnificent sight. Here were no glittering uniforms nor brave banners of silk. The long column of thin, sun-tanned men, marching in perfect cadence but without swagger, could not fail to delight the professional onlooker, yet I doubt whether a layman would have appreciated its true significance. As for me, I do not recall ever having felt greater pride. Pride, not in myself, except as a cog in a smooth-running machine; but in my company, my battalion, my organization—as fine a body of real fighting men as can be found in the world.

At the review, the troops were served with a good meal—with extra rations of wine—and given their liberty for the balance of the day. All of the officers joined the General at luncheon, while in the evening there was a great dinner for the Staff. The bars, for once, were down. Most of the men had imbibed rather freely by the time the evening had set in; nor were any officers to be descried who failed to uphold their honour as six-bottle men. Let me add, parenthetically, that while many of my English and American friends had assured me that no Frenchman is to be found under the influence of intoxicants, these otherwise enlightened persons can never have had the good—or ill—fortune to observe French troops in Morocco on a holiday.

It is the custom, in garrison towns, for each

unit to patronize its own restaurant or café—its own in the sense that the soldiers of a given regiment prefer to annex a single private establishment—rather than to divide their allegiance between several. General Poeymirau, when the Staff dinner had drawn to a lengthy and convivial close, suggested that his officers should accompany him in making the rounds of these resorts, and, nothing loath, we followed in his train.

I remember visiting at least four of the regimental establishments, at each one of which there was much toasting, speech-making, and cheering, before we brought up at the Café des Négociants, a favourite resort of the N.C.O.'s. Here we stopped for some time, while a grizzled sergeant-major regaled us with ribald ditties, and assiduous waiters plied us with wine of the country. I have no means of recollecting the number of additional cafés visited during the remainder of the evening.

I was relieved from Staff duty a few weeks later, and received an assignment as instructor at a machine-gun school, held for officers fresh from France. This kept me occupied for about six weeks, during which period General Poeymirau became ill and returned to France. There he died, shortly afterwards, a gallant officer and a *grand seigneur*.

I applied for Christmas leave and, receiving it, proceeded to Tangiers to meet my wife and son who had come out to pay me a visit. We remained in that pleasant city for some days and then went up to Rabat where I succeeded in renting a bungalow for my family. Although I continued to be stationed at Meknes I was able to spend my week-ends in Rabat, and thus the winter passed under pleasant auspices.

On May 1, 1924, I was ordered to proceed to Fez, there to take command of the mounted company of the Second Regiment of the Legion. These mounted companies—there is one to each regiment—are famous for their ability to negotiate long forced marches, and are used particularly for desert campaigning. There are two hundred and fifty men in each of these organizations, and one hundred and twenty-five mules, picked for their sturdiness and speed. Each mule carries the kit of two men while the soldiers themselves alternate between riding and walking. In addition to the ordinary armament of infantry, the mounted companies are equipped with four heavy machine-guns and four automatic rifles. They are respected and feared by the tribesmen, for it is almost certain that any depredation committed while one of them happens to be within striking distance will bring down swift and drastic retribution.

The city of Fez, far less Europeanized than the other large Moroccan towns, presents a romantic picture as one approaches from Meknes. Flanked by high mountains to the north and east, it crouches at their feet, turreted and bastioned, aggressive in its very passiveness. Nearing the ponderous gates, one is impressed by the strength and durability of the thick walls which have endured from medieval times, never pausing to consider that modern artillery could pound them to pieces almost at will. Above, minarets and towers pierced the blue, and morning and evening the high-pitched chant of the muezzins floats eerily down over the housetops. It is all so enchanting, so reminiscent of the story-book Orient, that one feels personally affronted when, upon entering the gates, one is assaulted with the rankest stench imaginable—an odour at once defying description and beggaring emulation. I am quite certain that no other town, the world over, can enter into serious competition with Fez—at least in this particular department.

The Sultan maintains a large palace in Fez, as does General Chambrun, commander of the northern district. It was to this rambling and once magnificent structure that I reported upon entering the town; but as the General was absent upon a tour of inspection, I was able to complete the formalities with more than the usual dispatch, and thus join my new company which had just returned to the garrison after a period of duty at Enjil.

Upon the evening of the first day, I gave a dinner party for a few friends, selecting as a place of entertainment the Hôtel Transatlantique. Dinner over, my brother officers conveyed me to the equally famous Hôtel du Maroc, a resort set upon one side of the Place de Commerce in the heart of the native city. This hotel is well known to all officers serving in Africa and is, more or less, a rendezvous for Légionnaires. One is almost certain to meet old friends there, and many have been the reunions at one or another of the long bars that traverse the huge common room. The patronage is cosmopolitan and colourful in the extreme. *Demi-mondaines* infest the place, yet it is quite proper to dine there with one's wife. Every uniform known to the French military service may be seen there at one time or another, while the flowing burnous of the wealthy Arab merchant is to be descried, more than occasionally, swaying about the dance floor to the tune of the latest—for Morocco—American fox-trot.

Here, upon that first night, I revived old friendships—made during the previous year's campaign—and embarked upon many new ones. Spirits ran high, and I am afraid it was very late ere I departed in search of my quarters in the garrison.

The next few weeks were spent in hard work. We had received a warning order from Headquarters to make ready for field service—the usual summer task in Morocco. I remember that I had considerable difficulty in selecting suitable mules to replace those outworn by service, in drawing fresh equipment for my men, and in getting the administration of my new command in working order, all within the time limit assigned me. In this work I was assisted by my new commanding officer, Colonel Rollet, who had a fatherly affection for the mounted company, which he had commanded years before. Rollet, a little black-bearded chap, had commanded the Legion during the war and was adored by officers and men. He was a very humane man, given to visiting the garrison hospital with cigarettes for the sick or wounded, and in general comported himself in a manner quite unexpected in a gruff old soldier of the Legion.

This new company of mine was made up of men of every conceivable social position, of every profession, and of forty-eight different nationalities. During the days spent at Fez, I learned that they were the very devil when let loose in the native quarter, my non-commissioned officers—nearly all Germans—being not a whit better than the others. I did not bother them, however, so long as they appeared each morning fit for duty; and I soon found that, from a purely military standpoint, they were nearly perfect.

The Légionnaire, after all, leads a dull, hard life for nine months of the year. A little relaxation, when in garrison, is to be expected.

To the east and north-east of Fez runs the river Ouergha—the stream given so much prominence during the campaign against the Riffi—and from this vicinity disquieting rumours began to drift.

The Ouergha, you see, roughly divided the French zone from the Spanish, and on the far side of the stream the armies of Abd-el-Krim had been, for many months, engaged against the forces of Spain. The division, however, was rather a peculiar one, in that it provided that those tribes who obtained water from the river—regardless of the side upon which they lived—were under the French mandate, while those who lived too far beyond the stream to make use of it in this manner were considered to inhabit the Spanish zone.

During the winter of 1924, the hordes of Abd-el-Krim, flushed with their continued success against the Spaniards, began to rob the friendly tribes situated on the extreme limits of the French zone. Whether they had need of cattle and provisions or were just a trifle out of hand made no difference to their victims. It was enough that men, working in the fields, were shot or cut down at their labours, that women were carried off as hostages, and that cattle—most precious of all possessions—were commandeered to feed the armies. The Kaids banded together and appealed to Maréchal Lyautey for protection.

So it was that we received our marching orders and prepared to cross the Ouergha, with the intention of making a more or less peaceful penetration of the lands beyond the river. At the edge of the zone we should, following out our usual plan, establish a strong chain of outposts.

Two groups were dispatched upon this mission, one starting from Fez and the other from Taza, in which again we followed a usual custom. We began the march north at three o'clock on the afternoon of May 21st.

The valley of the Ouergha is, naturally enough, more fertile than the country below the Middle Atlas. The tribes are agricultural, after the manner of lowland people, and rather less warlike than the mountain men. Thus we proceeded unmolested, except by the broiling heat, and reached the mountain of salt called Tissa, at the end of two days. The third day found us at the river bank—at a miserable native settlement known as Ain Aicha. Here we established contact with the Taza group and remained in bivouac for several days. The expedition now numbered in the neighbourhood of ten thousand troops, counting the irregulars or Goums which are under the command of political officers. These Goums are made up of one hundred and twenty-five infantrymen and fifty cavalrymen, all in native costume but armed by us. They are recruited from the friendly villages and make, under favourable conditions, valuable allies, although, during a setback, they are apt to melt away like snow.

We found the Ouergha River to be a broad, muddy stream, fordable in places, but undrinkable. Even the animals refused to touch it, and we were obliged to find water for them in the hills. Our encampment, though, pitched in a grove of ancient oaks, was pleasant enough, and we were sorry to leave it on the twenty-seventh to fare forth into the dazzling sunlight.

On the morning of the twenty-seventh, both groups forded the river and advanced across the plain beyond. My mounted company, together with a Goum, formed the right flank guard. Although no trouble was anticipated, we took all the precautions customary to old African campaigners, and proceeded as if entering upon an attack.

The country, despite the heat, was really beautiful. The tribesmen utilized the Ouergha and its tributaries to irrigate their fields and orchards, so that, in addition to wheat and corn, pomegranates are not an uncommon sight. We passed through, or round, numerous native villages. The male inhabitants stood about in small groups, not hostile, apparently, but aloof, as if holding judgment in abeyance. Thus we went forward for thirty kilometres and joined the main body at five in the afternoon. The main body, upon halting, had immediately set about fortifying the encampment. The site selected, upon high, rocky ground, commanded the country for miles around, but, owing to the hardness of the baked earth, it was impossible to dig in. The infantry threw up low stone walls around their positions, while the gunners were forced to forgo even that slight protection.

By this time, General Chambrun was holding audience for a deputation of native Kaids who awaited him with a lengthy list of complaints. There was a great deal of salaaming; compliments were exchanged; then, and only then, was our commander able to get down to the real business of the day.

It seemed—we learned this later, of course, at a meeting of officers—that Abd-el-Krim had formed a habit of exacting tribute from the lowland villages in exchange for his dubious protection. Finding that the levy was met promptly (for the lowlanders stood in wholesome fear of his raiders) Krim decided to collect oftener and in greater quantities. Finally, when the size of the tribute precluded all possibility of the farmers' being able to make ends meet, they rebelled. This, apparently, was exactly the move for which Krim had been waiting. Strong raiding parties swept into the villages, burned the crops, stole the cattle, and carried off the more comely women. Not content with this, they entered the mosques and stole the priceless prayer rugs, the most cherished possession of the Mohammedans. At this crowning insult the followers of the Prophet—fatalists though they were—could endure no more. Dextrously reconciling themselves to his Christianity they dubbed General Chambrun "Defender of the Faith" and implored his protection.

The General assured the Kaids of our cooperation, impressed upon them that we had no wish to interfere with their religion or customs, and promised to establish a strong chain of outposts in the troubled zone. Then, as the darkness closed down swiftly—like the avenging hand of Allah—the deputation retired, apparently well satisfied with their day's work.

As for us, our labours had just begun. Ahead of us stretched the fertile plain, from the extreme limits of which rose the long blue line of the Riffi mountains. The Staff spent the next few days in selecting strategical positions for outposts, and then, in a burning heat which often reached 120 degrees, we started work on the outer walls.

My mounted company—the only unit of the Legion which remained with the expedition—

furnished specialists for the engineering work. There were a number of masons, stonecutters, surveyors, and artisans of every variety in the organization, and these proved invaluable in directing the colonial troops in the work of erection.

The Ouergha, thirty kilometres to our rear, changed direction some distance above the point where our crossing had been made, and thus ran, for some distance, at right angles to our front, although far to the right of our actual position. In order to secure our flank from a possible surprise attack, the General established a small camp on the right bank of the river, where it turned. The garrison consisted of one native battalion, one battery of mountain guns, and forty of my mounted company, all expert machine gunners.

Our occupation continued uneventful for some days, the work proceeding apace. Then, on June 6th, if I remember correctly, during luncheon, we heard a burst of firing on the right. We paid little attention at first, but, as the firing increased in volume, the luncheon party broke up. It was obvious that our camp on the right bank had been attacked.

We were in communication by heliograph, and our first move was towards our signalling detachment. Soon the message was flashed—"We are attacked in force—position surrounded—enemy estimated at eight hundred—we can handle situation without help."

The General directed the besieged force to call for reinforcements if necessary, ordered our artillery to open up harassing fire, and we returned to luncheon. The firing continued until four in the morning and then ceased.

At 5 a.m., I formed the ammunition section and marched up to relieve the detachment. I arrived at seven o'clock to find the fight over and the men in high good humour at having beaten off a vastly superior force. We had lost about fifteen men and two officers, while the tribesmen, attacking from the open, had suffered heavy casualties. Owing to the native practice of carrying off their dead, we were unable to make identifications, and to this day it is not known whether the attackers belonged to Abd-el-Krim or were simply a band of young tribesmen out for a lark.

I replenished the food and ammunition and returned to the base camp carrying the dead, among whom was the only Dane, besides myself, in the mounted company.

The heat continued unabated for several weeks. Referring to my diary I find that the temperature at 8 a.m. was seldom below one hundred and ten. So we worked, and sweltered, and cursed our luck, and were bored.

By July 1st, we had, by dint of backbreaking effort, erected the outpost chain, and our task was for the present completed. It is interesting to note here that every one of these outposts fell during Krim's surprise attack in 1925.

CHAPTER TWO

ON the fifth day of July, the mounted company received orders to return to Fez for eight days' rest. We set out through the heat, over terrific country, and arrived at the garrison city at the end of the third day.

Heat or no heat, we were supremely happy. Eight days in which to do nothing except the necessary fatigue! Eight days in which to drink and carouse and sleep! Ah, sleep is the ultimate luxury to the early-rising Légionnaire.

Personally, I recall those eight days without pleasure. My men, to be sure, were enjoying themselves after their own fashion; but that fashion is one calculated to harass and be-devil the poor company officer. Broils with the natives; quarrels over women—although, heaven knows, these last were not much to quarrel about—and pitched battles with the military police. Men absent without leave; men lying drunk in low native dives; men stabbed or bashed on the head—I welcomed the marching orders that came in on July 16th. We were to leave Fez on the following morning *en route* for the Middle Atlas, there to take over an outpost sector.

At midnight, then, on July 17th, together with a squadron of Spahis and a line company of the Legion, we marched out. Once again, as on my first experience with the Étrangères, my men swayed in ranks. And once again I marched the liquor out of their systems.

We halted at 6 a.m. at the village of Sefrou, a charming settlement on the banks of a small stream, with scores of palm trees growing about the houses, and many luxuriant gardens. Sefrou is a political post, presided over by a French major, and is settled largely by Jews. We rested there through the day and until two o'clock the following morning, when we again took the road, marching thirty kilometres to Tazouta.

The country became rougher now as we approached the frontier, and the road led gradually upward. Tazouta was the last friendly town on the route. We remained there for a day and then began the final leg of our journey, sending out a strong point and flank guards, and taking up our usual campaign formation. After a long forced march, we reached the key post at La Kelaa and there relieved a battalion of the Legion which had held the sector for eighteen months.

The battalion commander was overjoyed at our arrival. After a year and a half in these isolated posts, his men were half mad with solitude. There was a great celebration and everyone had rather more than enough to drink. The luncheon held for the officers was talked about, throughout Morocco, for more than a year.

The next day I went forward with my company to take over the sector of Ich Lerouaf. The outposts in this sector ran along the crest of a ridge, and all were visible from the ramparts of the central position which I occupied. In the valley, to our front, wound a broad, shallow stream, while, beyond, the terrain rose sharply to form a long, continuous crest.

Each morning the réveillé was sounded at five and black coffee was served to the troops.

Then the trumpeter at the central post mounted the ramparts and blew the advance, the shrill notes carrying for miles and echoing among the empty hills. With the first note of the trumpet, the gates of all the posts opened simultaneously, to give egress to detachments of Spahis. These advanced, under a barrage of machine-guns trained on the opposite crest, and took up positions on the high points, there to ward off possible attack or to report the advance of any considerable force of hostile tribesmen.

Thus protected from surprise attacks, the troops marched to the river bank, stripped off their uniforms, and bathed. This, together with the drawing of water for cooking and drinking purposes, took up the greater part of the morning. At 11 a.m., the troops returned to the posts, there to take up positions on the ramparts while the Spahis, in their turn, withdrew from the high points. Once all detachments had returned to the several posts, the roll was called and the gates closed down. *La soupe* was served them, and at one o'clock the morning's performance was repeated, this time in order to protect the fatigue detachments which were sent out to cut firewood, bury rubbish, etc. At 6 p.m., the Cossack patrols were withdrawn again, and this time the gates were closed for the night. Evening *soupe* then, after which the men were free to go—nowhere. Do you wonder that some of them became mad?

It was a great event, in those days, when one of my lieutenants was able to visit me for luncheon. Early in the morning, my signaller would report that Lieutenant C—— wished to report to me with the week's ration returns. I replied, invariably, with an invitation to lunch—which the Lieutenant, of course, expected—and then sent for my cook and mess orderly. Great preparations followed. One would have thought that my visitor was to be at least a full General, or perhaps even a Field Marshal. Yet it was this very show of interest in comparatively trivial things which kept men sane.

By the same token, when there was no work to be done, I worked my men furiously, causing them to perform all manner of arduous and entirely unnecessary labours. Just so long as they grumbled and cursed their commander,

I knew that everything was quite all right. Had they been bored or inert I should have had reason to anticipate the dreaded *cafard*.

After a fortnight at Ich Lerouaf, the squadron at La Kelaa was relieved and sent back to Fez. The departure of the squadron left me as senior officer of the district, necessitating my taking quarters at the central post, a move which I was able to make without a single regret. La Kelaa was more spacious, more comfortable, closer to civilization, and in every way preferable to the outlying posts, and I anticipated having a much better time there.

To La Kelaa supplies were delivered from Fez, while we, in turn, transported them to the advance posts. In addition to flour, canned goods, bacon, etc., whole herds of cattle were sent us, it being impossible during the winter rains to reach us at all. The cattle remained at La Kelaa, in a special stockade built for them, and individual beasts were delivered to the outposts when requisitioned. Thus we were kept in fresh meat in a country where it would have been impossible to transport even synthetic foodstuffs during six months of the year.

The fact that there were several outposts between La Kelaa and any known hostile tribes did not make it safe for us to deliver supplies unless protected by a strong guard. Infiltration is not at all difficult in a territory so lightly held, and the natives easily pierced our lines at night in order to waylay wagon trains. It was true, on the one hand, that the tribesmen could not storm our small fortresses —at least, not without suffering terrific losses. On the other hand, it remained equally true that we were unable to prevent their roving whithersoever they wished under cover of darkness. When a supply train left La Kelaa for one of the advance posts, it was necessary to make a start at daybreak. We sent out a strong advance party, guarded our flanks and rear carefully, and pushed ahead at a great rate of speed in order to arrive at our destination before noon. Half-way to our objective, we were met by a party which had been sent back from the post to escort us or, if necessary, to clear the way for our progress.

Once arrived at its destination, the train was unloaded, the men served with a hasty meal, and after a brief breathing space the return journey was begun. It was only by dint of great speed that the base post could be reached before darkness closed down; and we had no wish to be ambushed in the night simply because we had delayed too long over the midday meal.

I made it a habit to accompany most of the supply columns, partly owing to the fact that the responsibility for their safe passage was mine, and also because the trips broke the monotony of my daily life. Two posts in particular I enjoyed visiting. The first was the key post of the Tizi Anni sector, commanded by a Captain Grassart, who enjoyed a wide reputation as a cook. This officer, when apprized of my coming, always baked a delicious cake—from a recipe of his wife's—mixing the ingredients with his own hands and superintending the actual baking. The other was the political post of Skoura, presided over by Lieutenant Le Blanc. Skoura was a garden spot in the midst of the wilderness, well watered and under careful cultivation. The Legion had lost several officers there, as the Berbers seemed to take special delight in raiding the settlement. Le Blanc had a really wonderful native cook who prepared the most delicious kous-kous—a dish composed of chicken, barley, chopped olives, etc.—to be had in Africa; and the long ride over the sun-baked hills was well worth while when one considered the kous-kous at the journey's end.

On the fourth of September, I was conducting a supply train bound for the key post at Ich Lerouaf. When still some three or four kilometres short of our destination, I heard firing from the vicinity of the right flank guard. Putting my horse to the gallop, followed by a detachment of Spahis, I soon arrived upon the scene to find two of my four men killed, the others wounded, and all four rifles stolen. There was not a native in sight, and although we scoured the vicinity, we did not come across even a track. My poor men had walked into an ambush. The natives, rising from their positions behind rocks, fired a volley at a range of fifteen or twenty feet, dispatched two of my men with their long knives, and disappeared completely, all in the space of not more than three or four minutes. Do you wonder that we took elaborate precautions?

Life was soon fairly well organized at the

post of La Kelaa. My first consideration was for the proper victualling of my men, and to this end I secured the services of an Arab who journeyed, once a week, to Sefrou, where he purchased fruits and fresh vegetables. The stonecutters and masons built an excellent kitchen, with two fine ovens, and our cuisine was really extraordinary for a company in the field.

It may appear to the reader that I dwell overmuch upon food in my descriptions of outpost life; that I am something of a gourmand. Nothing, as a matter of fact, could be further from the truth. Yet we had but few creature comforts in those trying days, and food came to take on a tremendous significance. The Légionnaire, in his spare hours, is not much given to sports or games. He does not play football or indulge in other forms of athletic competition. Rarely is he to be found gambling. All this renders it exceedingly difficult to keep him contented, and I found, through long experience, that a well-fed Légionnaire is apt to keep himself out of mischief.

The winter rains began in October, and as

all of the outposts had received eight months' supplies, life became, if possible, even more dull. As the month wore on, dreary day succeeding dreary day, I fell ill with fever and, finally, had to be moved to the base hospital at Rabat. Upon my recovery, I was relieved from duty with the mounted company and assigned to Maréchal Lyautey's staff as intelligence officer. Thus began the pleasantest days I spent while in service in Africa.

CHAPTER THREE

MARÉCHAL LYAUTEY, as Resident General of Morocco, filled the most difficult of diplomatic posts with credit and dignity. He was the one man in Morocco who held, at once, the confidence of the natives, the Sultan, and the home government. He has done more for the French cause in Africa than any living man.

The Maréchal received his appointment as Resident General in 1912, in which year the French Government signed a treaty with the Sultan. The general idea of this agreement was that France, acknowledging the Sultan through a Resident General, should take upon herself the task of establishing order in the country, rearrange its finances, and assist in the development of its vast natural resources. Lyautey had a profound knowledge of the native, had carried on several colonial wars with vigour and distinction, and was noted for his general executive ability. Nevertheless, the task with which he was confronted was really gigantic.

In the first place, most of the outlying tribes were in open rebellion against the Sultan's government. They refused to pay any taxes whatsoever, defeated the government troops which were sent out to enforce order, and spent the rest of the time in quarrelling among themselves. The country's finances were in a deplorable condition. Of decent roads and other means of communication and transportation there were practically none. The whole of Morocco was up in arms, one petty tribe pitted against another.

In spite of this, the Maréchal attacked his problem with unfailing energy, using tact when tact was needed, and the Foreign Legion when things had gone beyond the limits of mere talk. In the two years before the outbreak of the World War, he accomplished wonders. He established order throughout the greater part of the country, built roads, railways, and ports, and saw to it that the native farmer or manufacturer received fair prices for his goods.

Then came the World War, and with it an order from the home government to evacuate the whole interior of Morocco, to keep only the coast cities occupied, and to release several regiments for duty in France. This the Maréchal refused to do. Not only did he fail to evacuate one inch of territory, but sent home at the same time twice the number of regiments the government had requested. One is forced to admit that, after but two years, this was a truly remarkable achievement.

As Resident General, the Maréchal held a dual responsibility to the Sultan and to the French Government. He had also two cabinets—military and civil—with which to carry on his work.

The Sultan, on the other hand, is not by any means a mere figurehead. Muley Hassan, a man of fifty-odd years, is responsible for the adjudication of all questions relating to the natives, and these he handles with considerable acumen and ability. In addition, he was consulted by the Maréchal in all matters of policy, and as each man held the other in sincere respect, they were able to work together in harmony.

When I took up my duties as a member of his Staff, the Maréchal was at least seventy years old. At an age when most men have reached their dotage he worked with great rapidity, day and night, seeming to sleep not at all. In the Residency at Rabat (it is really a very beautiful modern palace) he lived amidst considerable pomp and splendour, surrounded by enormous black house orderlies in blue and white *képis*, yet never seemed to notice the almost kingly magnificence of his entourage. He was, in the best sense of the phrase, a true *grand seigneur*.

The Sultan also lived in a great palace, not far from the Residency. Here he held daily audiences and worked nearly as hard as the Maréchal himself. Muley Hassan likes the French rule, as it has brought his wild country under control. Without it he would not have been able to accomplish a single one of the reforms in which he professes such great interest.

One of the most interesting sights of Rabat is the Sultan's weekly visit to his private mosque. Each Friday, mounted upon a beautiful white Arab horse and surrounded by his black guard of eight hundred men, Muley Hassan takes this means of showing himself to his people. The Sultan, despite his cleverness, is not much to look at; but the guard is one of the finest sights in the world. Imagine eight hundred enormous black men, all of them more than six feet three inches in height, attired in brilliant red uniforms trimmed with gold. They are perfectly trained by French instructors, although the company officers are natives, and form one of the most compact standing armies the world over.

My work as an intelligence officer was not too arduous, with the exception of one or two confidential missions in the Spanish zone, and I found that I had ample time in which to take part in Rabat's social life. My wife and son again came to live with me, and all through the winter I enjoyed a pleasant respite from the rigours of African campaigning. It was the lull before the storm.

With the approach of spring, ugly rumours began to drift in from the vicinity of the Ouergha. The tribes on the northern front were getting restless, and it was reported that Abd-el-Krim—who had lived in amity with Maréchal Lyautey for several years, and who alluded to the Resident General as " Protector of the Faith "—had been threatening the tribes under the French mandate.

CHAPTER FOUR

MOHAMMED-IBN-ABD-EL-KARIM, better known to the world as Abd-el-Krim, was a petty chieftain, the Kaid of the three Riffian tribes who inhabited the mountains north of the River Ouergha. An ambitious man and a good soldier, he was educated at the native university in Fez and learned campaigning under the old bandit Raisuli. Serving as one of Raisuli's trusted lieutenants for several years, he was thrown out of employment when that worthy sold himself for much Spanish gold. Krim was infuriated at his master's treachery to his people, and thus decided to do a little campaigning on his own—reasoning, no doubt, that if it was worth millions to the Spanish crown to buy Raisuli off, then he, Krim, could do worse than follow his erstwhile commander's precept.

At any rate, there was Krim, backed by a

compact force of trained fighters; and it seemed to him that organized banditry was not only more profitable but preferable in every other way to the drudgery of farming or tending flocks. Possibly he was correct.

Little by little, as time went on, Krim's power increased. It was not long before he led a small army, rather than a bandit gang, and had dreams of driving the Spaniards into the sea. The world knows how close he came to accomplishing his ambition.

Krim's first big stroke was his attack on Raisuli, the renegade. That worthy, since his capitulation to the Spaniards, had lived in retirement in his mountain stronghold—a sort of warden of the northern marches. Here he maintained a strong bodyguard, a houseful of wives, and some five million pesetas. In addition, there were no less than seventy thousand stands of small arms, a proportionate amount of rifle ammunition, together with several modern light field pieces, hundreds of machine-guns, and other war material. A prize indeed!

One fine evening, Abd-el-Krim, aided by his brother Sidi Mohammed, swept down on

Raisuli's fortress, put the garrison to the sword, and captured the treasure. With the news, tribesmen flocked to his standard, and before long he was defeating the badly trained Spanish troops with great regularity. His army grew: his victories became more and more frequent; and the whole Spanish zone, with the exception of a few coast cities, came under his dominance.

Up to this point Krim had conducted his campaigns brilliantly and with rare good sense, while his unofficial diplomatic relationship with Maréchal Lyautey did him no harm. To be perfectly candid, the French did not care how often Abd-el-Krim beat the Spaniards. Had it not been that England feared to allow France full sway in Morocco, there would probably never have been any Spanish zone at all, and France was not unmindful that crushing defeat might mean the complete withdrawal of the Spanish forces.

Thus matters stood in the spring of 1925 when the rumours of Krim's approach to French territory began to trickle through to us.

I do not know what actually happened in

the Riffian councils of war when it was decided to penetrate the French zone. It may have been that Krim's successes had gone to his head, and that he considered himself unbeatable—a supposition that I very much doubt, running contrary, as it does, to the characteristic actions of a very sagacious man. Rather I think it was that the fighting men were drunk with victory. They had routed one European army, defeated it time and time again. Who, then, were the French to block the path of the soldiers of the Prophet? Krim, probably, acquiesced when he saw that they would attack in any event, and in spite of his orders to the contrary. Of course, later on, there was a great deal of loose talk about autonomy, and the natural granary of the Riffi, etc., when, as a matter of fact, the tribe had never been anything but autonomous. As to the granary, that belonged to the tribes who cultivated it. The Riffi have no claim to it now, nor had they ever.

Although the three Riffian tribes formed the nucleus of his standing army, Krim's forces, at the outbreak of hostilities against the

French, had been greatly augmented by the enlisting of scores of other tribes. Some of these came voluntarily, in the hope of having a good fight with plenty of looting afterwards, while others were impressed into service as Krim's armies passed through their territories. They had the alternative of joining Krim or having their lands and homes laid waste. Who can blame them for their decision?

The three personal tribes, however, made up the finest of Krim's troops. Well-trained in the art of modern warfare by German adventurers, they were, in addition, fanatical in their devotion to Krim's cause. When it is considered that these men can live and fight well for twenty-four hours on a handful of dates and a mouthful of water, that they were unencumbered with supply trains, and that they fought in a mountainous country with which they were absolutely familiar, it is no slur upon the French colonial troops to say that one Riff tribesman was equal to three or four of them. Even the Foreign Legion met its match in the Riffi. I can extend to them no higher praise.

PART III

CHAPTER ONE

IN April, 1925, then, it became apparent that we should have to keep a sharp watch on our outposts beyond the Ouergha River. Where all had been peaceful a few months previously, now gathered the clouds of war. Fatigue parties from the various outposts were ambushed by comparatively large native forces; and, on the nineteenth, I learned from another staff officer, who had just returned from the north, that the Riffi, forming three great *harkas*, or phalanxes, had entered the territory of the Beni Zeroual tribe, burning and laying waste as they advanced.

We sent a squadron of bombing planes to harass the advancing army while we laid plans to rush all available troops—there were not very many—to the northern front.

By April 22nd, we knew for certain that this general advance was no mere raid. The Riffi had reached our line of outposts, stretching from the Atlantic to points north of Fez and Taza, and had calmly set about digging themselves in, after the most approved manner of European armies. It was at this time, too, that our intelligence service learned that Krim's chief of staff was a Colonel Von Taunberg who had served brilliantly with Mackensen during the advance of the German armies in Eastern Europe. With Von Taunberg were numerous other German adventurers, and these turned out to be the men who so efficiently handled Krim's artillery during the subsequent fighting.

By April 25th, the situation had changed for the worse. During the nights, the Riffi slipped between our outposts, cut all our lines of communication, and compelled many of the heretofore friendly tribes to go over to them. Maréchal Lyautey cabled Paris for additional troops and, with those already available, formed three relief groups, one at El Kelaa des Sles under General Colombat, another at Taza under Colonel Combay, and the third, under Colonel Friedenberg, at Tisa.

But, quickly as we worked to marshal our

forces, we were not in time. Two days later, the Riffi made a concerted attack on our outpost line and completely surrounded it. Our garrisons were cut off from the outside world. On the twenty-ninth, Colombat's group was ready and advanced west to sweep the enemy from the vicinity of Fez El Bali. He had seven battalions—between three and four thousand men. We heard nothing of him for several days.

On the morning of the thirtieth, we received information that four or five thousand Riffi had crossed the Ouergha and were marching on Tisa. And then again silence.

On the evening of May 2nd, my wife and I dined with the Maréchal at the Residency. Just as we were about to enter the dining-room, a courier arrived with further news. Chambrun, at Fez, sent word that all of the posts in his sector were completely surrounded. He said, further, that Colombat's group had engaged the Riffi in pitched battle and had sustained great losses, that Colonel Combay had been defeated at Kifane—north of Taza—and that Colonel Friedenberg was about to attack. He requested the Maréchal's permission to evacuate the entire outpost line should he deem it necessary. This permission he did not receive.

We went on in to dinner, but the Maréchal sat silent throughout the meal. There were no more reserves, and he was fully aware of that fact. As we left the table, he ordered me to hold myself in readiness to accompany him to Fez in the morning.

Arriving at Fez the following day, we were met with further bad news. Krim, it seemed, had not yet used his shock troops, and was preparing, with these, to take the city. When it was considered that our own available forces were divided into three widely separated groups, each one of which was fully occupied at the time, there seemed no good reason why he should not be able to accomplish his mission, if such it was, and there was a general exodus from the city of merchants and other members of the civil population. Sympathy with Krim there might be among the native population, but none wished to leave his worldly goods about, a prey to the wild looters from the hills. It was a black day, the single bright spot being a telegram to the effect that twelve battalions of infantry and four batteries of field artillery had been ordered from Algeria—to arrive in a fortnight.

The following morning, fresh news of the fighting cheered us somewhat. Colombat's group had achieved a slight success which relieved the pressure on a few posts, while Combay had actually been able to effect a relief to the north of Taza. We were advised that Colonel Friedenberg was to push to the relief of the post Taourmat during the afternoon.

General Colombat had sent in a request for officer volunteers to join his group. He was badly in need of liaison officers, as he had been obliged to use most of the juniors of his staff to replace gaps in the line. I requested the Maréchal to release me from my duties on his staff in order that I might join Colombat, and he complied, ordering me to report that afternoon to General Chambrun, who was directing operations from his headquarters in the city.

Shortly after midday, I entered General Chambrun's headquarters, which was connected by wire with the front. In a large room, seated at a long oak table, were the General and his Chief of Staff, receivers glued to their ears. I saluted, and the General motioned impatiently for me to sit down.

Pinned to the wall opposite my chair was a map of the area in which the fighting was taking place, the locations of the various units marked out with tapes and coloured glass-headed pins, exactly as in a war game at some school of tactics. Between this map (the markings of which he constantly shifted upon fresh advices from the front) and the telephone, the General spent the afternoon. At four o'clock, after two hours of anxious waiting, word was received from Colonel Friedenberg that he had accomplished his mission and relieved Taourmat. The General brightened for a moment, only to exclaim angrily, as a report of terrific losses followed over the wire.

There had been no news from Colombat for some hours, and we waited, tensed, for his report. It was one of the most dramatic moments, I believe, in the lives of each of us. Finally, word came that Colombat had been stopped in his attempt to relieve Bibane. He begged reinforcements, and reported that the small garrison of the post continued to hold out, although badly in need of food, water, and ammunition. General Chambrun dispatched two fresh battalions from his almost negligible reserve at Fez, ordered Colombat to aid Bibane with his artillery, and sent several airplanes to attempt dropping food, munitions, and ice into the post. Shortly afterwards reports ceased coming in, and the General turned to me with an apology for having kept me waiting throughout the afternoon. As a matter of fact, it had been one of the most exciting days of my life, and I would not have exchanged the experience for untold gold.

For several days, General Chambrun used me at headquarters, and I was thus enabled to obtain first-hand information of the fighting in all sectors. On the fifth, Colonel Friedenberg had another small success, relieving pressure somewhat, and, on the sixth, several posts in the eastern sector were able to re-munition. There was a lull for twenty-four hours, and then, on the eighth, the reinforcements arrived from Algeria. This enabled us to send the last of our reserves to the front, and Colombat planned to push a column through to Bibane on the thirteenth.

That day we waited at headquarters with bated breath, while messages came in informing us of the battle's progress. For a while, it seemed that we were again doomed to fail.

The column attacking on the left was held up by the enemy at their first line of trenches. The right attack group broke through the lines, only to run into a heavy machine-gun fire which pinned it to the ground. Colombat, however, took a long chance, threw in his reserve upon the left flank, and broke through. He was able to resupply the post, carry off the wounded, and effect his retirement before darkness had set in. A brilliant action, but one far too costly to be repeated often.

A few days later, General Chambrun ordered me to accompany Colonel Naugés, his Chief of Staff, in the front, and we left, a few hours later, for General Colombat's sector.

We drove as far as the south bank of the Ouergha in a Staff car, crossed the military bridge, and then took a motor lorry to Fez El Bali where horses awaited us. At 5 p.m., we reported to General Colombat at the key post of Tafrant, where his combatant group was in position.

CHAPTER TWO

TAFRANT is situated some fifteen or twenty kilometres north-east of Fez El Bali, and is the base from which some of the hardest battles of the whole campaign were launched. A chain of hills lay to the north and west of the post, almost in a semi-circle, and on various high points, all visible from the key post, five outposts were situated, four of which were held by our troops and one of which had fallen early in the campaign.

To the north-east, about seven kilometres, stood the ill-fated Beni der Koul whose brave garrison perished so horribly some time later. Almost due north was Archirkane, at a distance of about five kilometres. Audour was parallel with Archirkane, slightly to the north-west, and again at a distance of about five kilometres, while Bibane, the charnel house, stood almost to the west of us, six kilometres away. South of Bibane the ridge ended in an escarpment, and it was from this direction that all relief expeditions were launched.

On June 23rd, General Colombat's force consisted of what remained of seven infantry battalions and five batteries of seventy-fives. At Fez El Bali he had a battery of howitzers. The post of Bibane, which he had relieved three times, was entirely surrounded by the Riffi, and two valuable battalions, which he had left behind with the garrison to reinforce and entrench the post, were unable to break through Abd-el-Krim's lines and thus rejoin the main combatant group.

As the work of these battalions had been completed, and as they were badly needed elsewhere, the General decided to attack again in order to relieve them. The garrison proper, of course, had no alternative but to remain at the post.

We informed the forces at Bibane, by heliograph, to expect our attack on the morning of the twenty-fifth. On the twenty-fourth, the General, with his staff, prepared his plan, issued a warning order, and informed the other outposts of his intentions. Colonel Naugés was to act as advance guard commander, while I accompanied as liaison officer.

Before dawn, then, on the twenty-fifth, we marched out, the advance guard two battalions of the Legion and one mountain battery strong, and the entire force numbering not more than two thousand men. At six-thirty, we arrived at the jump-off position, a shallow depression, just south of the spur below Bibane. Some three hundred yards ahead lay the front-line trenches of the Riffi which we had been ordered to carry by assault.

It was a grey morning, and quiet—ominously so. Our barrage, the attack signal, had not begun. There was a great deal of nervous adjusting of equipment. A man swore softly and brought down a volley of whispered curses on his head. The Legion was in a blue funk, the nameless fear that precedes battle. I would not give a sou for soldiers who failed to act similarly on the eve of an assault.

The barrage opened with a crash. Junior officers leaped to head their platoons. There was no noise that could be heard over the crack of the seventy-fives, but here and there an arm waved and the grey battalions deployed to disappear into the mist.

We followed, the Colonel and I, close upon them. The firing had grown so heavy now that one advanced in a sort of coma, the shattering din suspending all thought for the time. The enemy machine-guns must have opened up then, for the ground, as we walked on, was dotted with sprawling Légionnaires. Otherwise I should not have noticed it.

We had reached their first line. Bayonets flashed, here and there, as the mist lifted. We were holding our own—we had them! Then our own barrage closed down upon us. . . .

That trench became a shambles. With devilish accuracy our own shrapnel burst over our heads, killing Légionnaire and Riffian alike. I sent at least a dozen runners back, and finally the barrage lifted, but by this time the enemy machine-guns had the range and we were unable to move.

Up to this time, our losses had been enormous, but now, although we were committed to a fire-fight for the time being, the casualties were less heavy. To our left front stood a low, thick-walled stone house, crowded—after the German fashion of "nesting"—with enemy machine-guns. We concentrated our attention upon this miniature fortress but, although we shelled it for hours, the machine-guns continued to sputter.

As it was obvious that we could not advance farther until the house had fallen, I managed to communicate with the commander of our mountain battery, requesting him to bring his fire to bear upon it. He not only complied with my request but brought his guns into the trench where, at a range of less than two hundred yards, he fired point-blank at that obdurate blockhouse, and with no discernible effect.

Finally, an ammunition group came up with a supply of hand grenades. With these we hoped for better success. First, we launched a bombing party at their second-line trenches—some seventy-five yards to our front—but it failed to reach the enemy line, owing to those devastating machine-guns. Then we attempted to bomb the house proper, but with no more success. With each failure, the enemy flung taunts at us, threatening various forms of torture to any prisoners taken, and boasting that they knew all of our plans almost as soon as we did ourselves—which may have been true. Realizing, then, that further attempts at carrying the blockhouse by assault were useless for the time being, we contented ourselves with maintaining a rapid rifle and automatic rifle fire, and waited to learn what had happened to our main attacking group.

This group had, in the meantime, deployed on our right, where it met with a similar brand of resistance. Krim's infantry, plus a highly organized system of entrenchments, was almost unbeatable, and it looked, for a while, as if the whole assault were doomed to failure.

On the extreme right—which was, of course, the enemy left of line—stood a blockhouse similar to the one which held us up. A battalion of the first regiment of the Legion tried to take this by frontal assault, as well as the trenches alongside it, but with each attempt the attacking group was swept away before it had fairly started. Section after section leapt the parapet and rushed to the attack. It was no use; the men went down like wheat before a scythe.

Major De Lande, who commanded this battalion, became furious at the loss of his men. Twelve of his officers survived, and these he called together. Then followed one of the most extraordinary military feats that it has been my fortune to witness.

Serving each officer with a sack of grenades, the Major distributed them at intervals along the line directly opposite the enemy trench and blockhouse. At a given signal they leapt the parapet as one man and advanced at a brisk run, hurling grenades as they came within range of the Riffi. The trenches, at this point, were not more than fifty yards apart, so that it could not have taken the Major and his daring party more than ten or twelve seconds to traverse it.

Almost at once, it seemed, they came to close quarters. The enemy trench fairly spat fire, but the officers, instead of melting away, carried on. Then the grenades began to take effect. The grenadiers, every one of them experts, hurled their bombs with incredible speed and accuracy. The trench-lip seemed, in spots, to rise up, only to crumble immediately into new and unfamiliar shapes. The

Major hurled bomb after bomb through a window at one side of the blockhouse. A wall bulged outward and then crashed. Nothing could have survived within.

The remnants of the battalion ceased their covering fire then, without command, and followed the assault. They reached the trench to find the twelve officers—who, by some miracle, had not suffered a single serious wound—in complete possession.

It had been proved, now, that the Riffi were not invulnerable. How or why the twelve officers survived that awful fire has always been a mystery, but it is possible that the continuous assaults unnerved the enemy to the extent that he was unable to stem this last attack through sheer lack of will. When men keep coming and coming, wave upon wave, daunted not at all by slaughter, it must occur to the defenders that these are not soldiers at all but inexorable fate.

Fate or otherwise, the success on our right bolstered our waning morale. A few minutes later, a half battalion of the Legion—fresh troops—came up to reinforce us, with orders to carry the blockhouse by storm. It is unfortunate that one successful charge does not necessarily imply another.

The senior captain of the reinforcing contingent decided to take the blockhouse with one company. We increased our fire for a while to keep the enemy's heads down, so that the assaulting force should have an opportunity to get fairly started. Immediately before stepping over the parapet, the captain remarked to me that his men would either take the blockhouse or remain upon the field. They rushed to the advance, then, and the machine-guns opened up with redoubled fury. The captain fell after having gone forward for perhaps ten paces. Some of his men fared better, and one lieutenant reached a point not fifteen feet from the enemy guns before he collapsed like a pricked balloon. Wounded men, attempting to crawl forward, twitched under the impact of fresh bursts of fire, then lay still. Not one returned.

The second fresh company poured a withering fire into the enemy trenches. Several of them mounted the parapet as if to charge the blockhouse unaided, but were dragged back by officers who had managed to keep their heads. One corporal crawled seven times into

No Man's Land, returning each time with a wounded comrade. On the eighth attempt he was killed.

The battle continued for some hours without much change. We launched no more sporadic assaults, but saved our energies for a general attack. I returned to General Colombat with a report on the situation, and he decided that our final thrust was to be made at one-thirty in the afternoon. In the meantime, we were to bring all of our artillery, some of which had been ranging on other targets, to bear on the blockhouse and the trench that stretched to its right. The supply train was brought as far forward as was compatible with comparative safety, and at one o'clock all was in readiness.

At the decided moment, we rose out of our trenches and marched methodically, and without undue haste, over that hard-fought ground. Nothing, this time, could have stopped us. We poured into the enemy trench like a tidal wave. The blockhouse crumbled under the impact of our grenades. Although the Riffi did not retreat, we took no prisoners.

It took us another hour to reach the post, fighting each step of the way. We threw out strong detachments on each flank to prevent the enemy from enveloping our column, yet, before we had progressed more than a few hundreds of yards, we found ourselves engaged in a hot rear-guard action. As we drew nearer the post, the Riffi closed in on us, and when the gates banged shut on our last man, we were completely surrounded.

The survivors in the garrison proper numbered fifty-four men. Sergeant Bernis was in command, with two other French non-commissioned officers as his section executives. Then there were four French gunners, a French signalman, and forty-six Senegalese infantrymen. They were overjoyed to see us, but fearful that this would be our final attempt at a relief. It took us some two hours to re-munition and supply the post. Then we formed for the return.

As the gates opened, Sergeant Bernis saluted his captain—who had been with our attacking force—and said, simply, "Good-bye, sir, I am afraid we are to be sacrificed." The Captain embraced him, we moved out, and the gates slammed shut behind us.

The return, although accomplished under a

heavy fire, was not so hard fought as had been the advance. When we had gained the trench line again, a strong rear-guard was detached to cover our retirement across the lower plain, and this, in turn, made a hasty withdrawal under our covering barrage. As we drew nearer to our base at Tafrant, we again heard firing on our right. A Riffi force had advanced across the plain during our absence, and had spent the day in harassing the garrison. We were just about to deploy again to teach the beggars a lesson when four squadrons of Spahis advanced at a gallop from behind a hill and put them to rout. After a hard day, it was a pretty sight.

CHAPTER THREE

AFTER roll-call, we totalled our casualties and found that we had lost eighteen officers and more than five hundred enlisted men—one man in four of the entire attacking force. Obviously, we could not afford to relieve Bibane again unless we could remain in permanent possession of the heights, and this was impossible while our strength was so low. By keeping our main body at Tafrant, in a position to strike out in any direction, we stood a reasonable chance of being able to save Fez. With our whole force—and it would have required that—at any one of the posts it would have been comparatively simple for Krim's army to outflank us and, after falling upon our rear, to continue almost without opposition to the outskirts of the city. We knew that Bibane was doomed, and knowing, were downcast.

Later that evening the signal blinker flashed

a message that Bibane was suffering a heavy attack and requesting artillery support. The firing continued unabated through the night and we realized that the life of the post could be measured, almost, in hours. When the morning sun had risen sufficiently to make use of the heliograph, the signalman again requested relief. We flashed back, "Hold on a few days longer," and cursed ourselves for the false encouragement.

Krim must have realized, by now, that we had no intention of allowing our force to be withdrawn again from its strategic position, for each night stronger forces of his riflemen ventured out upon the plain to make us miserable with their harassing fire. One night, the quartermaster, who lived alongside me, was killed while sleeping in his tent—this was on June 1st. On the third, Sergeant Bernis again requested relief, stating that he had lost eight more men. The wounded, he said, were suffering horribly, and his garrison had not slept for forty-eight hours. We fully realized their awful plight, but signalled, nevertheless, that relief was coming soon. We lied, and we knew it. And so, I imagine, did the Sergeant.

On the fourth, the Riffi began closing in around the post, but our artillery was busy elsewhere and could not assist the gallant defenders materially. On the fifth, we saw shrapnel bursting directly over Bibane and realized that Krim had brought up his German artillerymen. This was at 9 a.m.

At ten, I accompanied General Colombat to our artillery observation post, where we remained throughout the day. From there we could watch the enemy drawing closer, ever closer, to the outer walls, while our guns pounded for all they were worth. At four in the afternoon, the Riffi swarmed out of their trenches and rushed the walls. The heliograph flashed, despairingly, "*Poste fichu!*" Then came the final signal, never to be completed. We stood, breathless, repeating every letter as it was flashed—"S-E-R-G-E-A-N-T, Sergeant B——" and they scaled the walls, hundreds of them!

The General clenched his teeth. His face livid, he swung round to the artillery commander and said, "Now! let them have it." In a trice every gun switched to the post and, though some of our brave men probably remained alive, pounded it to bits. The General wept.

Next morning, we shelled the Riffi as they carried off such material as could be salvaged from the wrecked post. It was a most depressing sight.

CHAPTER FOUR

ONCE Bibane had fallen, we knew that Audour and Archirkane were to come next. The troops released from the siege would strengthen materially the forces surrounding the other posts, and it was only a matter of time until they, too, would be taken.

General Colombat telephoned to Maréchal Lyautey advising that the threatened positions be evacuated now rather than that their garrisons be left to the tender mercies of an overwhelmingly strong enemy, but again permission was refused. Whether or not the Maréchal acted wisely in refusing to abandon the post line is not for me to say. But it is difficult to stand by, helpless, while one's comrades are being butchered.

On June 7th, Krim's forces made a thrust at our lines near Ouezzane, and General Colombat led a flying column to relieve the defending troops. This left Tafrant under the command of Colonel Pompey, an old soldier who had small patience with red tape, and one used to taking matters into his own hands. The Colonel observed, at once, that Audour and Archirkane could not hold out much longer, and heliographed orders to evacuate, if possible, at two o'clock the following morning. He had not much hope of the garrisons winning back alive, but knew that, in a running fight, they stood at least some chance of evading the massacre that was inevitable if they continued to hold on.

Audour was held by fifty men under the command of Lieutenant Franchi. There were thirty men and one sergeant at Archirkane. Both commanders signalled that they understood our message, and asked for our artillery support during their withdrawal. The enemy, however, seemed to understand our heliograph—although the messages were in code—as well as did the beleaguered garrisons. Later, we learned that they flung taunts at the defenders, threatening them, as usual, with torture, and informing them that they had intercepted our instructions.

The firing continued unabated throughout

the day and into the evening. We watched the progress of the battle as best we could while daylight lasted, standing-to in our own trenches after nightfall, ready to send a rescuing force into the plain should either of the garrisons successfully carry out their attempt at breaking through.

We received blinker signals up to nine o'clock, after which there was a lull in the firing. Somewhere between nine and ten there came the sound of a terrific explosion from the direction of Audour, followed by absolute silence. Our signals flashed in vain after that, for we received no answers. Could anyone be alive in the post? Again and again we flashed: "Send up a green rocket if you get this message," but to no purpose. It seemed almost incredible that they could have broken through the lines, yet firing had ceased at Audour. Either the post had been blown up or else the Riffi had stormed it. We had almost lost hope of ever seeing our men again. Nevertheless, instructions were given the men on our front lines to be careful to avoid firing into the refugees, should any return, and our vigilance never relaxed.

Those of the officers who were not actively engaged stood in a little knot that night, and discussed the garrison's chances. Towards 1 a.m., someone declared that he heard a noise on our right front. We paused to listen and, sure enough, there it was again—the rattle of bayonets! Our hopes rose then. The artillery opened up a drum fire on the Riffi lines. Another half-hour passed, and still no sign of our returning men. We ceased fire and strained our ears to listen.

There it was again! Closer this time—not more than a few hundred yards off our front—the rattle of equipment. A captain was sent out with fifty men to reconnoitre in the direction whence the sound had come. Finally, at 1.30 a.m., they returned—with the garrison intact. The young Lieutenant Franchi was the last man to drop into our front-line trench.

I ran back to the post and awakened Colonel Pompey to give him the good news. He, poor man, pulled on his tunic and stepped into the courtyard of the post proper just as Lieutenant Franchi marched in at the head of his little band.

"Platoon, halt! Present arms!" came the

command. Colonel Pompey stopped dead in his tracks and returned the salute automatically. From his expression one would have supposed that he had suddenly been confronted by a detachment of ghosts. Then, realizing the significance of what he saw, and appreciating the perfect discipline and magnificent swank of the ragged band, a smile broke over his tired face. He congratulated the men, embraced Lieutenant Franchi, and ordered the last of the champagne served out to the detachment.

We gathered around Franchi in the mess room and, tired though he was to the point of exhaustion, he related the story of his escape. He had seen, he said, the capture of Bibane as if from a seat in a theatre, and had realized then that he had but a slim chance of ever getting through alive. He explained that the reason for the continued fierceness of the enemy attacks was due to their elaborate system of reliefs. Every forty-eight hours fresh troops entered the trenches, effecting the change with European precision, while the retiring body returned to a back area for rest.

Among the troops who besieged his outpost

the Lieutenant said that he recognized many familiar faces, men who had traded with his troops but a few months before and who were perfectly aware of the general layout of his fortifications. These led the jeers and taunts which followed every exchange of signals, seeming to have a perfect knowledge of our code, though where they had picked it up was more than any of us could say.

After receiving his orders to abandon the post, the Lieutenant set about devising a means to divert the enemy while his men made good their escape. He cut two small breaches in his outer walls, to his right and left fronts, and placed his two field pieces in them, depressing their muzzles so that they were aimed point-blank at the enemy. Then, after dark, he cut a larger breach in his rear wall, facing us, through which he intended to effect his retreat. About fifty or sixty yards to his right rear was a large shell crater where his men were to take refuge before embarking upon the final dash for safety.

At about eleven o'clock, the enemy could be observed creeping closer to the walls as if to rush, and Franchi ordered his men out to the shell hole, remaining, himself, until the last. The rush came then, and Franchi, timing the whole thing perfectly, fired both his field guns point-blank into the charging mass, wreaking fearful execution upon the closely bunched enemy. These were the explosions we had heard.

The discharge of the guns held up the attack for a few seconds and, in this time, Franchi made good his escape, joining his men in the shell crater. Despite their discipline, the Riffi delayed to loot the post after finding the birds had flown. The garrison left their shelter and, with the aid of a few grenades, broke through the thinly held line at the rear. Their progress was rapid for the next few minutes, but they knew that pursuit was inevitable.

In order to avoid detection, Franchi ordered his men to unload their rifles, fearing that the noise of firing would give his whereabouts away and bring down a hornet's nest about his ears.

When attempting to cross a narrow stream which lay between his position and Tafrant, he was attacked by a roving detachment of Riffi, but was able, by sharp work, to cut his way through at the point of the bayonet. This was the first of the noises we had heard. And here he suffered his only casualties—one sergeant wounded and one private killed. The sergeant refused aid when it was offered him, and told the rest to go on. He knew enough, Franchi said, to save a bullet for himself.

Shortly after crossing the stream, they met a rescuing detachment—which did no rescuing after all—and the rest we knew. The Lieutenant remarked, as an afterthought, that his garrison had subsisted, for the last week, on one meal and one cup of water per day. Then he slept.

There was, however, no sleep for our garrison. We had heard nothing from Archirkane up to now, and in the general excitement of receiving the survivors from Audour had almost forgotten that a second withdrawal was in progress. Not so the gunners. At 3 a.m., they opened up again, this time attempting to lay a box barrage around Archirkane in the hope of cutting off pursuit by the enemy. They kept it up for ten minutes, then ceased firing.

At about three-thirty, we heard a sharp burst

of rifle-fire from the general direction of the post. The silence that followed caused our hopes, raised by the earlier success, to sink. We could not expect to be so lucky twice in the same night. I remember turning to a companion and saying, flatly, "They are caught."

Indeed, it seemed that my prognostication was justified, for the silence remained unbroken for another half-hour. Then our artillery opened up again to pour shells into the post proper. Shortly after this retaliatory effort had ceased, we heard another burst of rifle-fire, the staccato popping interspersed now and again with the deeper crash of hand grenades. Closer and closer came the sounds. We heard a sharp challenge from our forward listening post, and a few moments later the rattle of equipment and the tramp, tramp of weary feet assured us that at least some of our men had won their way through.

As a matter of fact, the sergeant in command of Archirkane, after breaking through the enemy lines, had separated his command into three groups, each one of which took a different route to Tafrant. He had calculated wisely, as it turned out, for, having used his full strength when a shock effect was needed to break through the lines, he had made pursuit more difficult by splitting his small force into details. All had been pursued, but each one had been sufficiently strong to delay the enemy who, perforce, had also been obliged to separate his command. Here was one instance, at least, when it was tactically sound to divide a small force, for the enemy, in full strength, would almost certainly have overwhelmed our men had they been held together in a single unit.

Each group had lost a man or two, and almost all had suffered wounds more or less severe. But they came through.

The sergeant arrived with the last element of his command and made a brief verbal report to Colonel Pompey. He had, it seemed, been unable to make his escape undetected, so, taking the bull by the horns, had charged with hand grenades under cover of our barrage. Once through the lines he had, as before stated, divided his command and trusted to luck. Although obliged to carry on a running fight almost the whole of the way back, his plan had worked itself out with a remarkable degree of success. Forlorn hopes do not always fail.

The following day was quieter. We observed the Riffi swarming like ants over the abandoned posts, but refrained from firing, as our supply of shells was not overplentiful. As neither of the escaping garrisons had been able to put their field pieces out of commission, we anticipated that we were in for some shelling. They had, however, buried their extra fuses, and it appeared that the Riffi had not been able to locate these highly essential articles.

The German gunners, apparently, were employed elsewhere along the front for, at about nine-thirty that night, the Riffi turned the guns on us, minus fuses, and dropped a few dozen duds among our tents which were pitched on a reverse slope behind the post. They did no further harm than to annoy us, and our own guns, opening up, soon silenced them.

It is interesting to reflect upon the contempt in which modern troops hold duds. After all, a dud, while it does not explode, is the equivalent of the old-time solid shot, and is capable of doing considerable damage; yet men who are used to fire pay absolutely no attention to a shell which does not explode, and go calmly about their business without pausing to consider that these flying projectiles are exceedingly lethal provided they score a direct hit.

The enemy seemed to have grown weary of playing with the captured guns, and we settled down that night for some much-needed sleep. I had scarcely composed myself in my small tent when I was awakened by a terrific roar, followed by curses and screams of pain. The enemy, having bracketed our position with duds, had found the fuses and now, without warning, began to fire for effect. The remainder of the night was hideous, for their fire continued with unabated fury and uncanny precision. Our own attempt at counter battery work was without result, for they had shifted their gun positions and carefully screened the flashes. We could only pound away, taking dubious satisfaction in the knowledge that our gunners were sending back more than we received.

At dawn, after the rolls had been called and the wounded evacuated, Colonel Pompey called the officers together and told us that it had been decided, now that the outposts were abandoned, to hold Tafrant with six companies of infantry and a few guns, withdrawing the remainder of our force for service elsewhere. Scarcely able to believe that the key to Fez was to be risked to the defence of so small a force we prepared, nevertheless, to take up the march again, thoroughly glad to be quit of so dismal a position.

Twelve hundred pack mules were sent up that morning from Fez El Bali. We struck tents, loaded up equipment, and marched out at 2 p.m., throwing out a strong cavalry screen to protect our left flank from an attack from the Bibane escarpment. As our column got clear of the posts, shells began falling within the walls. The Riffi were jubilant now, and considered their game already bagged.

Out in the plain our position was none too pleasant. We marched all afternoon, our route about paralleling the enemy line, under hot shell fire, while the Spahi flank guard became engaged, almost at once, in a series of running fights. At last we reached Fez El Bali, our bivouac for the night, and hastened to ascertain the condition of the garrison at Tafrant. The signallers informed us that the post had been completely surrounded within an hour after our departure, and that, even now, the Riffi were at work on an elaborate trench system.

In a way, it was a good thing for us that their attention had been diverted to Tafrant. Our own position at Fez El Bali was extremely precarious, hemmed in, as we were, by the hills, and with scarcely any natural protection. Sounder strategists than the Riffi would have ignored the smaller game to sweep down upon our force in the hope of dealing us a crippling blow. Once we were out of the way, Fez would have been at their mercy, and it might have been possible for them to make an advantageous peace. As it was, however, the Riffi ran true to form, finding themselves incapable of forswearing the easy prize for the more difficult and consequently greater one. Natives, I have found, are oftentimes highly successful at adapting European tactics to suit their own peculiar demands; but European strategy is beyond them.

Encumbered with mules, baggage, and wounded, we were not much better than a mob that night at Fez El Bali, and it took us a full twenty-four hours to bring order out of chaos. The men were weary with a more than physical weariness. They had sustained such hardships, with scarcely a single victory —certainly no decisive one—to bolster their morale, that they carried on in a sort of semi-coma. Fez was never so weakly defended as upon that night.

We had set up a camp upon arriving, and I dined in my tent with a Lieutenant Tabouille who had charge of the transport. As night closed down, the blinker messages from Tafrant became more and more disquieting. Tabouille was as nervous as a cat, for his younger brother had been left behind at the post in command of a native company. At about nine o'clock I accompanied this officer to a slight elevation from which we could observe the flashes of the guns and read the signals for ourselves.

It was a weird sight. The post was literally

ringed with fire, so continuous was the cannonading. Every minute or two a flare would burst over the enemy trenches, outlining his positions in a ghastly blue-white light which faded almost as soon as it came. Above it all, the single telegraph blinker—dot dash, dash dot dot—recorded the progress of the fight, "We are hard pressed. Can you send help?" Dot dash, dash dot dash!

The fight raged with undiminished fury until 2 a.m. Then it ceased, abruptly.

We signalled, at once, to ascertain the losses. Tabouille clutched my arm as the message came back, slowly, "One . . . Lieutenant . . . killed! Four sergeants. . . ."

Tabouille let go my arm and ran for the signal tent. "Call them back!" he shouted. "Name, name, *name!*"

The signaller flashed out the question, but the blinker was needed for more important matters. To that message we received no reply.

Tabouille, of course, was beside himself by this time. He was certain of his brother's death, insisting that everything pointed to that fact. I took him back with me to my tent and attempted to reason with him. "Look here," I said, "there are twenty lieutenants at Tafrant. Don't be ridiculous. Your brother is perfectly safe."

"He is dead, my little brother," Tabouille replied wearily, and, throwing himself upon my bedding roll, slept.

At 5 a.m., I was awakened by an orderly from headquarters. "We march out at seven, sir. Will the Captain inform the Lieutenant that the transport accompanies the column? And there is a message, sir, from the Lieutenant's brother. Oh, yes, sir, he is quite safe."

CHAPTER FIVE

WE marched that day some twenty-odd kilometres to the railhead at Kolen, there to assist in the defence of that base and to aid with our guns the defence of another outpost known as Beni der Koul. This post was situated on the crest of a ridge, very much as had been the ill-fated Bibane, and it too could not hope to hold out much longer. I had been there but a day, however, when I received orders to rejoin General Colombat at his new base, Ain Defeli.

Taking the narrow-gauge military railway at Kolen, I arrived at Ain Defeli after a sweltering journey of some seven hours. Actually, I believe that I could have walked the distance in less than that time. There I had good news, for a message had been received from Tafrant that the enemy had made a final assault and, after sustaining heavy losses, had withdrawn his troops.

For some days now there was little activity along the front. Both sides had grown weary of the almost incessant fighting, and each suffered from the excessive heat of the tropic summer. On the thirteenth of June, the Staff embarked in a series of motor-cars and travelled farther left to Ouazzane. Maréchal Pétain and Premier Painlevé had flown to Morocco from Marseilles and had come to inspect the front.

Now that the home government had begun to take an interest in our situation, we felt somewhat heartened. It did not take Maréchal Pétain long to recognize our plight and to recommend that heavy reinforcements be dispatched from France at the earliest moment possible. The result of this visitation from the High Command was felt almost at once, and fresh troops poured in to relieve the decimated battalions which had held the lines for so many weary weeks.

As for myself, I did not realize that my Moroccan campaigning was drawing to a close. Just after the Maréchal's visit, I was assigned the task of laying out a new defensive system at Ain Defeli. I worked at the plans for several days, arranging also to fortify the railhead near by, and it was while completing these labours that I heard the story of the fall of Beni der Koul, the last of our outposts to succumb to Krim's attacks.

It appears that the post commander, a young sub-lieutenant named La Pierre, fresh from the military school at St. Cyr, had at last received orders to evacuate his position. Unfortunately for himself and for the few surviving members of his garrison, the post was, by this time, quite surrounded. The Riffi had established themselves in strong entrenchments and seemed prepared to starve him out.

Knowing perfectly well that he could anticipate no relief for at least several weeks, and having but three days' supply of water in the butts, La Pierre heliographed to headquarters requesting that a message be sent his parents in France informing them that he was well and quite safe. He held out, then, for two or three days longer, beating off several attacks with seeming ease. Then his machine guns went out of commission. Once more he signalled: "Six men alive. When may I expect relief?" It is probable that he received an evasive reply for, two hours later, he blew the post up, perishing, presumably, in the explosion.

On the eighteenth of June, I was ordered to Fez once more to instruct some of the reinforcing battalions in the use of the machine-gun. Here I remained for another two months, sweltering in the awful heat and turning out machine gunners in droves. The news from the front grew steadily more encouraging, and the lines were now firmly held. No one could predict, at that time, how long it would take us to break Krim's power, but we knew that, by the following spring, at the latest, we should have him on the run. He had put up an extraordinary fight against some of the finest troops in the world, had caused a first-class power to tremble for the safety of one of her most prized colonies; now it was but a matter of time until the eagles should stand upon the ruins of his villages.

It was towards the end of August, I believe, that I became ill. An old wound had been giving me trouble, and the hard work under the tropic sun undermined my powers of resistance. I kept on for as long as I could and, one day, found myself occupying a cot in a base hospital. From there, when I became convalescent, I was moved to Casablanca, thence to Marseilles and Paris with an order for six months' sick leave tucked safely away in the pocket of my tunic. I had seen Morocco at her best and at her worst; my experience with the Foreign Legion had gone beyond my most romantic expectations; I was content, for the time being, to rest.

THE END